D1412037

I love Robert Herber's new book, The Partying God. *Robert is a great story-teller whose writing is so authentic. This book is a refreshing read that inspired me to be more and more radical for God! When you read this book, expect to be stretched and changed by the God who loves a party. There is one caution, however, to be aware of. When you start reading* The Partying God, *you will not be able to put it down.*

LARRY KREIDER

International Director of DOVE Christian Fellowship Int'l
Author of over 35 books

Jesus was a man of joy above all others. From years of knowing Robert, I can say that his daily life is a reflection of this deep conviction: God is throwing a party in heaven and on earth, and He has invited you to be a part of it. In The Partying God, *my dear friend Robert Herber not only shares how he has experienced this joy, but how you can have it too!*

JIMMY SEIBERT

Pastor, Antioch Community Church, Waco, TX
President, Antioch Ministries International

I have enjoyed and benefited from the ministry of Robert Herber. He is prayerful, faithful, and committed to loving people. This new book by him is a welcome arrival. I am excited to read it.

MAX LUCADO

New York Times Best-selling Author
Preacher, Oak Hills Church, San Antonio, TX

Partying God? Really? Robert Herber tells it honest and from the heart. We all want to know what God is really like. What spirituality is about. Robert's relevant stories and conversational style is like talking with a friend. And he makes sense. You will have a hard time putting this book down once you start!

FLOYD MCCLUNG

Director, All Nations, Cape Town, South Africa, & Author

Party on & God Bless!

Robert Herber

THE PARTYING GOD

DISCOVERING THE GOD OF
EXTRAVAGANT CELEBRATION

ROBERT HERBER

With ROBERT FULLER

THE PARTYING GOD

Copyright © 2015 Robert Herber.

All rights reserved. No portion of this book may be reproduced, stored in a retrieval system, or transmitted in any form or by any means—electronic, mechanical, photo-copy, recording, scanning, or other—except for brief quotations in critical reviews or articles, or as specifically allowed by the U. S. Copyright Act of 1976, as amended, without the prior written permission of the publisher.

Published by Clear Day Publishing, a division of Clear Day Media Group LLC, Franklin, TN. Cleardaypublishing.com. In association with Lux Creative {theluxcreative.com}.

Scripture quotations are taken from The Holy Bible, New International Version®, NIV® Copyright © 1973, 1978, 1984, 2011 by Biblica, Inc.® Used by permission. All rights reserved worldwide.

ISBN: 978-0-9909719-1-7

Cover Design: Benjamin Monson –
            shepherddesigns@gmail.com

Contributions from Samara Myers

Printed in the United States of America.

Library of Congress Control Number: 2014959546

To my wife, Stefanie:

You have been my best friend, a tireless co-laborer, faithful counselor, and the most fun person to be with. God couldn't have given me a better companion for this incredible journey!

To my kids:

I love you guys so much. Your laughter fills my heart. I delight in how you are always up for a new adventure. What a joy to take the gospel to the nations with you! May you be so convinced of God's extravagant heart of celebration that you run after Him whole-heartedly all of your days.

CONTENTS

PARTY LIKE YOU MEAN IT

The summer before seventh grade something happened to me that felt like winning the lottery. It changed everything. How I saw the world. How I thought about life.

My cousin moved to town from California.

His name was Jeremy. He was two years older and stood on the cutting edge of fashion. He was the first person I ever saw with sun bleached hair hanging over one eye, which he'd flip to the side for effect. He didn't wear the dull colors so common in Texas fashion, but showed up in neon, shining in all his blinding glory. He wore Vans. And not just any Vans, but the ones with no shoelaces, checkered in black and white.

He was the embodiment of cool.

Lucky for me, he was the new kid in town, which meant I was his only friend. So, despite my lack of flowing hair, glowing apparel, and cutting edge footwear, we hung out almost every day.

I'll never forget the time he invited me down to my uncle's house. The place had a detached garage that had been renovated into a den of awesomeness. It was the ultimate bachelor pad, complete with a huge television, gaming system, and even a pool table. There's no telling how many hours we spent cloistered up there. We lived it up. Big time. I even remember the songs that blared through the stereo.

One of them was David Lee Roth's hit, "Living in Paradise." This dates me, I know. But could there have been a better song? The lyrics still take me back:

This must be just like living in paradise.
And I don't want to go home.

I thought to myself, *this is it.* I have arrived.

As we reveled in entertainment bliss, my cousin started talking about the parties he would go to in California. It sounded like a dream world. I'd only seen what he described on TV. People actually went to things like that? I couldn't help but listen with wonder. But then he started describing the drinks he had had. Then the girls he'd hooked up with. I got a little fidgety. A tad uncomfortable. I mean, I was a Christian. These things were not supposed to happen.

"Hey ..." I muttered awkwardly. "Aren't those things wrong? I mean ... I'm a Christian. I don't think I'm supposed to do that kind of stuff."

The moment those words left my mouth my cousin's face dropped. He tilted his head and looked at me like I was the dumbest person in the world.

"Robert," he said, "if God is so good, then why would he want to keep me from having fun?"

I stared back at him in silence.

"If God is so loving," he continued, "why in the world would he keep these things from me?"

As I tried desperately to formulate an answer, my mind was struck with a memory I had of church: I am twelve years old, sitting in a pew. I'm surrounded by men in crisp suits and women in floral dresses, all eyes fixed on the stage where our kind and scholarly pastor approaches the pulpit.

"Today," said the pastor with a warm smile. "We are going to study the Tabernacle."

He then produces a transparency and places it flat upon an overhead projector, shining a diagram of the Old Testament house of God on a ten-by-ten screen for all to see. The pastor clears his throat and begins with an itemized breakdown of its architecture.

The acacia wood.

The dugong curtains.

The interwoven tapestries made of mixed fibers.

I remember sitting there, lulled lazy by his monotone voice, and thinking to myself, *I couldn't possibly be more bored.*

And so, as was normal for any preteen on the planet, I began to devise strategies to pass the time. I made up a series of games with my fingers. I fiddled with my calculator watch. I drew. I passed notes when my parents weren't looking. I even tried to see how many times I could pop my knuckles during one service.

Through this experience, and many more like them, I came to the conclusion in my juvenile mind that church was altogether dull. A place to be endured like a temporary jail term. And thus I assumed Christianity was boring as well.

Staring blankly back at Jeremy, my heart started to pound. All my years of sitting in pews and listening to pastors drone on about tabernacles hadn't prepared me a single iota for a rebuttal. My twelve-year-old brain went reeling. Why wouldn't God want me to have fun? Why wouldn't God give me everything good there is to have?

I believe we've all asked ourselves the same thing at some point or another. While I was unprepared for Jeremy's point of view, I don't think such questions catch Jesus off guard at all. In fact, I think it's one of the main reasons he told the most famous parable in the Bible. We find it in Luke chapter 15:11-32. Most of us know it as the Prodigal Son story. Let's start from the beginning:

"There was a man who had two sons. The younger one said to his father, 'Father, give me my share of the estate.' So he divided his property between them. Not long after that, the younger son got together all he had, set off for a far away country and there squandered his wealth in wild living."
- Luke 15:11-13

There is something within all of us that craves a "far away country." Let's call it the sin nature. We dream of the "greener grasses" of pleasure and our so-called freedom. We imagine ourselves so much happier when we can do whatever we want. But this deception, if heeded, will destroy us.

When I first heard my cousin talk about the parties, the drinks, and his experiences with women, a seed was planted in my heart. A simple lie: Sin is better than a life of holiness. This lie grew and grew until its roots of deceit were entangled about me like a spider's web.

I kept on thinking to myself, *It's a bummer I became a Christian at such a young age because I'm going to miss out on all the fun.*

Hear me on this: I knew it was good to eventually become a Christian, since Christians go to heaven. And I wanted to go to heaven. I'd heard about that other place with all its fire and misery and weeping and gnashing of teeth. I for sure didn't want to end up there. And yet, I couldn't help but feel a tad cheated.

While so many enjoyed a lifetime of worldly pleasures, I would have to live my boring little goody-goody life. It would have been so much better, I reasoned, to just live my life and have my parties and girls and fun and then, right before I breathed my last breath on my deathbed, cry out, "Oh Lord Jesus, save me!" Then presto, I go to heaven.

But man, I would have lived a fun life!

Obviously, my understanding of God and His ways was positively atrocious. I thought He was holding out on me. I believed that He was keeping His best from me. But we must understand who God really is. If we begin to understand His character and His ways, the lies we believe begin to fade.

I want you to think about the most loving, extravagant, amazing dad you can imagine. The kind who wants to set his kids up for success, lavishing them with rooms to sleep in, schools to learn in, vacations to go on, and food to eat—not once, but three times a day and more. The kind of father who works his fingers to the bone and his mind to a pulp in order to provide above and beyond for the needs of his children. Now, take this image and multiply it by ten thousand and that's Father God. He created His children because He loves them. He made Adam and Eve because He loved them. You, the one holding this book in your hands, are loved by God and placed upon the earth as His child.

Think about the creation story in the Bible.

The first thing God did for Adam and Eve was bless them. He gave them the responsibility of ruling over everything, then gave them everything they needed to eat. It was a perfect situation. An existence unspoiled by despair and undiminished by lack. The Lord told them, *You are free to eat from any tree of the garden. But you must not eat from the tree of the knowledge of good and evil, for when you eat from it you will certainly die.*

If you know the story well, you know what's about to happen. Temptation enters in by way of the serpent. And this enemy, Satan, is still at it today. He still tempts us the same way he tempted Eve back in the garden, saying that there is more to be had beyond God's restrictions.

We humans so quickly assume that if we give our life to God, we lose our freedom, like mindless automatons trudging glumly through life. The enemy says that if we do what we want all the time, we're free. But nothing could be further from the truth.

The Bible says we shall know the truth and the truth shall set us free. But when we walk in sin, the Bible says we become slaves, controlled by the enemy. The Devil wants nothing more than to make us believe that God is a tyrant who will take all our freedoms away. But the Bible says clearly in John 10:10, *"The thief comes only to steal, kill, and destroy; I have come that they may have life, and have it to the full."*

So they had this garden, right? A paradise full of every awesome thing. Nothing held back. Nothing forbidden, besides the fruit of a single, solitary tree in the midst of thousands of others.

God gave a rule.

A parameter.

Does this make him cruel?

In our limited and carnal minds, prone to spiritual anarchy, the idea of rules often make us squirm. We don't want to have to do anything. We don't want to be restricted.

But can I tell you something?

We already like rules. No, we already love them. We can't live without them.

Rules and parameters are what help make life work.

It's illegal to drive full speed, or at any speed for that matter, down a busy sidewalk. Why? Because people would die at random and you would never feel safe taking a stroll. We like this rule; it makes sense.

Here's another one. We like that you can't smoke on airplanes. When the stewardess hands you your soda and little pack of peanuts, we like that the guy next to us can't blow a lungful of tobacco smoke in our faces. Don't we?

We like that it's illegal to steal. That it's against the rules for someone to snatch your purse or swipe your iPhone on the street.

Rules are our friends.

Because they protect us.

And that's why God sets up rules. It's not to keep us from being free—it's to protect us. Why did God forbid Adam and Eve from eating out of the one tree? Because if they did, they would die!

I don't know about you, but if there was something my kids were wanting to do—say, run across the street at rush hour with scissors—I would probably, I don't know, forbid such ludicrous behavior. They might cry and whine and go on about how cool the scissors are and how pretty the cars are. But I wouldn't cave in for a second. Because I love them. I positively adore them and want to protect them from danger.

Now back to Eden: the enemy, the devil, comes in the form of a serpent and tells a lie.

"Eve!" he hisses in the most snaky voice you can imagine. "Did God really say not to eat of any of the fruit in the garden?"

The woman answers, "We may eat of any tree in the garden, but we must not eat fruit from the tree that's in the middle of the garden. And we must not touch it or we will die."

"You will surely not die!" says the snake, with a flick of the tongue. "For God knows that when you eat it your eyes will be opened and you will be like God, knowing good and evil."

Eve gazes again at the delicious-looking fruit, thinks about what the snake had told her, then reaches up and plucks one from a branch. She takes a bite (forbidden fruit juice running down her chin). Then gives a bite to her husband, who has been watching the whole thing in silence like a buffoon. He eats as well, and the rest is history.

Okay. I have a deep theological and historical question. Put your thinking caps on. Act like you're Ivy League. Are Adam and Eve alive? Has anyone seen the first humans walking the earth?

Think about it.

Don't rush your answer.

NO! Of course no one has seen them—because they DIED! God gave fair warning, which they didn't heed, and they suffered the dire consequences.

Now, they didn't choke on the fruit and fall dead the moment they took a bite. But their disobedience set death in motion.

Satan tried to tell Eve that God was holding out on her. He tried to make sin look so much better than the paradise they had already enjoyed. But in the end, it led only to death.

After hanging with my cousin that summer, I got deceived. Spurred on by his insistence that I was missing out on all the fun, I started watching shows that were bad for me, with more and more violence, and deeper levels of sexuality. My mind was exposed to darker and darker things. I started hanging out with people I would have never been friends with before. I knew it wasn't right. I didn't care. I might not have gone off the deep end, but I abandoned my family's values. And as I spent more time with this new crowd, observing things I had never considered okay before, I thought to myself, *Why not? What's the harm in trying just a little?*

Observing the girls around me, I'd think, *Dude, she's hot. Wouldn't it be awesome to see what I could do with her?* I'm not talking about the big time stuff. Just a little bit. That's all. No big deal.

But you can never stop with just a little bit. We are never satisfied with a static measure of sin. Our fleshly appetites continually hunger for more. We approach a new "experience" we know to be sin, but choose to indulge anyway.

Liken it to getting into a pool of water for the first time. We gingerly stick a toe in and are exhilarated at the experience. We never knew how awesome the water was! How cool and wet and refreshing! Then, since we know it's sin, we walk away convicted.

But the moment we're tempted to return, we come back to dip a toe in once more. Problem is, we're no longer satisfied with just a toe-deep experience. So we step in further, all the way to our ankles. The same enraptured delight. The same pleasure and thrill. Then conviction and guilt, followed by the same dulling of the senses and lust for more. We go knee deep. Thigh deep. Waist deep. Chest deep. Neck deep. Head deep. All the way deep and then we drown.

All to keep the thrill alive.

It might have started with just a swimsuit issue. But then you go deeper into pornography. It might have started with just a puff. But now you're fully addicted to drugs. It might have started with an underage sip of beer, but now you can't stop drinking, no matter how hard you try.

This is the enemy's scheme. He will never just let you stick a toe in. His ardent desire is to destroy you. To enslave you. To ruin you in every way possible.

That's what happened to the prodigal son.

"After he had spent everything, there was a severe famine in that whole country, and he began to be in need. So he went and hired himself out to a citizen of that country, who sent him to his

fields to feed pigs. He longed to fill his stomach with the pods that the pigs were eating, but no one gave him anything."
- Luke 15:14-16

Not only did he lose his money—his entire inheritance—he lost his so-called friends, his reputation, even the chance for a decent meal. He ruined his life in wild living.

We are tempted on a daily basis to make the same choices: Do whatever you want. Live for yourself. Don't waste your life on a stingy, boring God.

We hear this lie, and sometimes our hearts quicken. Part of us wants to be the wild man. To be the rebel. There's something about it that seems mysterious and even risky. It smacks of adventure. But do you know what the Greek word for "wild" is? It's asotos, which means riotous. And believe me, you don't want to be caught in a riot. Riots are where people get trampled and die. Once we listen to our temptations, the cunning whisperings of the Devil, destruction awaits somewhere in the distance.

That's the enemy's end game. He is not your friend. Not your travel agent to a wondrous world of unrestricted pleasure. He's your executioner, leading you to the gallows. When you think you're simply going your own way, you're playing right into his hand. And that's exactly what the prodigal son did.

After he blows all his money on wild living, a famine strikes the land and he is left with nothing: not a bite to eat. This kid, once rich and in want of nothing, now scratches out a pathetic existence, so hungry he drools over pig slop. The once mighty son of a landowner now crouches in the mud, jealous of pigs.

Do not be deceived: this is exactly what the Devil wants to do with you. On the other side of every temptation is a trap door to destruction. He wants you destitute, devastated, and despairing.

And I was no exception.

Sinking deeper and deeper into sin, I eventually hit rock bottom. I'll never forget that night. Some friends and I broke into an old abandoned house carrying booze for an all night party. There was no electricity, so we ended up in the dark on the floor sipping our drinks. I grew increasingly uneasy as the night wore on. Every time a car passed on the road in front of the house, I silently panicked, thinking the cops were about to bust us. I remember being in the darkness beside my girlfriend, her pungent perfume wafting toward me, and thinking to myself, *Why in the world am I with this girl? And why am I with these people? I'm not like them. I'm not like this. I'm totally disgusted with myself. Is this the life I wanted? Is this all there is?*

Have you ever reached a point like this? Maybe your situation isn't as dramatic as mine. You're likely not stuck in an abandoned house where you could get arrested at any moment. But maybe you're scared and disappointed and disgusted with your life. Maybe you've been running after something to fill your voids and you've reached that inevitable point of questioning: Is this it? Is this all that life has to offer?

Thankfully the parable does not end in the pigpen. The story does improve.

"When he came to his senses, he said, 'How many of my father's hired servants have food to spare, and here I am starving to death! I will set out and go back to my father and say to him: Father, I have sinned against heaven and against you. I am no longer worthy to be called your son; make me like one of your hired servants.' So he got up and went to his father."
- Luke 15:17-20

The guy comes to his senses. It took bankruptcy, famine, and lusting over a pig's lunch to bring him to this point, but he came

11

to his senses nonetheless. Suddenly he remembered what it was like to live in his father's house, in his father's blessing. He realized that even his father's servants fared better than he was faring at the moment. I imagine him crouched in the mud at the edge of the pig farm, shaking his head in disgrace.

He knew he had only one choice left.

To return home.

Thankfully, I came to my senses too. My own eureka moment came from the mailbox. I got this letter from a guy named Garnett, who was my age and attended the same church. I'd never had much contact with the guy, so I opened the envelope without any idea of what I was about to read. The words struck me like a hammer:

Robert,
You call yourself a Christian. *But you live like a pagan. You're destroying your reputation and you're destroying your life.*
-Garnett

Oh, I was mad.

How *dare* this guy? Who did he think he was, writing me something so audacious and critical? Flushed with anger, I sat down at my desk, yanked out a pen and a piece of paper and wrote back with as much force I could muster.

Garnett,
Mind your own business! You don't know me. You don't understand me. You have no idea about my life.
-Robert

I folded the paper, stuffed it in an envelope, scrawled down his address and slapped a stamp on its face. I mailed it in such ardent rage I could hardly wait for the mailman to deliver it to his door. But no sooner was it sent off than I was struck with a tidal wave of conviction.

Deep down, though I was still mad at Garnett's boldness, I knew he was absolutely right. I knew my life had to change. I knew the road I'd been walking had never satisfied me for a moment, and was sure to lead to a dead end, if not to the edge of a cliff. I decided that night to give this church thing one more try.

So the next week I signed up for a youth retreat put on by my church. It's hard to believe one week I was partying in an abandoned house with my shady compadres, and the next, I was all cleaned up and walking into a room full of church kids. It took some getting used to. But sitting in my chair as the retreat began, I watched the main leader hop onto the stage and introduce himself. His name was Steve.

Up to that point in my life, I had never seen anyone so joyful. His face seemed to radiate every time he spoke to us about God. It was magnetic. Not only that, but the guy had just gotten married and could not stop talking about his wife and how awesome their marriage was. I thought to myself, *Now that's the kind of relationship I want!*

Throughout the entire weekend, he made us all feel so loved. From start to finish, it was an amazing time ... and at church! What? I can assure you, this was a first. Halfway through the weekend Steve cornered me and said, "Hey Robert, I want to get some time with you."

"Sure," I said, a little surprised to be so singled out.

"Let's go and grab some ice cream."

And so, just like that, we left the retreat for the nearest ice cream joint. I'll never forget what happened while we were gone.

Outside the ice cream shop there were these two gothic kids, all decked out in black, pierced all over, and gloomy as a storm cloud.

Steve nudged me. "Hey," he said. "Let's go talk to them."

A little flummoxed at his gall, I followed in silence as he approached the strangers and greeted them. "Hey guys!" he said. "My name's Steve. How you doing?"

They lifted their ashen faces and looked at him like he was crazy. Like his talking to them had broken a cardinal rule of Gothdom. But Steve was so kind and persistent in his questions that eventually, to my utter shock, they started to warm up to him.

How are you doing that? I thought. This is impossible!

And then he started talking to them about Jesus.

You can't do that! My mind screamed. These guys are GOTHS! They love the darkness and don't give a rip about God.

But right before my eyes, these kids totally engaged him in conversation. My jaw almost dropped. Here is this guy so full of joy and peace, talking to two kids so full of gloom and despair. The juxtaposition of light and darkness absolutely floored me.

As we walked off a while later, Steve turned to me and said something that changed the course of my life. "Robert, you're a leader. And you're either going to lead people straight to the pit of hell, or you're going to lead them to the joy of Jesus. It's time for you to choose."

I fumbled over my words, trying to respond rightly to his gutsy suggestion, but it was too much to take in so suddenly. I could do little but nod in agreement. My entire perspective on life had just been shattered into a million shards. As they fell down all about me, I looked at Steve and felt something deeper than I had ever felt before.

I wanted to be just like him.

I wanted to lead people to Jesus. I wanted his joy. I wanted his boldness.

That night I prayed to God, fueled by the day's experience.

"God," I said. "I want to walk with you. I want to follow you the rest of my life."

And thus began my journey home.

"While he was still a long way off, his father saw him and was filled with compassion for him; he ran to his son, threw his arms around him and kissed him. The son said to him, 'Father, I have sinned against heaven and against you. I am no longer worthy to be called your son.' But the father said to his servants, 'Quick! Bring the best robe and put it on him. Put a ring on his finger and sandals on his feet. Bring the fattened calf and kill it. Let's have a feast and celebrate. For this son of mine was dead and is alive again; he was lost and is found.' So they began to celebrate."

- Luke 15:20b- 24

Though the son knew he didn't deserve a thing, though he expected to lodge with the servants and had even prepared a speech to convince his father to take him back, the father sees him from a distance, runs to meet his son on the road and embraces him. Not only that, but he plasters him with kisses.

Really?

Grown men of that time, especially wealthy landowners, did not do this kind of thing. For one, they didn't run. Two, they didn't lower themselves to smooching on their sons for all to see. But this father didn't care about social norms. His son was back. He was alive.

As a father, I often have bad days. My kids are capable of all sorts of crazy behavior. But regardless, at the end of the day, you know what I do? I walk into their rooms, scoop each one of them up in my arms and kiss them all over their faces. They might squirm and laugh and act disgusted, but I don't care. I love them and I want to show them so.

Despite the prodigal's utter failures, his father loved him still.

He could have stood sternly on the porch as his son approached, waiting for the chance to lecture him. He could have demanded penance and a groveling apology. But that's not what happened. Not at all.

The father ran to him, embraced him, and threw him a party. A party? Yes, a party. A big, old-fashioned BBQ with brisket and ribs and succulent steaks! What else would you make from a fattened calf? He throws a robe of honor on the kid and makes him a virtual celebrity. It makes no sense at all.

So often when we try to talk to people about God, they shake their heads. "I don't want to talk about God. What has he ever done for me?"

But if they understood how good He was in this one verse, it would change everything. He's not sitting back in heaven ready to give his sinful children a tongue-lashing. No! He's waiting on the road, gazing off into the distance for our return, and when He sees you, He takes off running ... like a fool ... falls at our feet, and wets us with kisses, the ultimate sign of acceptance.

The world's party stripped the son of everything. His clothes, his money, and his dignity. What does the father do? He clothes him with a luxurious robe, puts a ring on his finger and sandals on his feet, and brings out the best of the best in his honor.

God's party builds you up.

The world's party tears you down.

God's party makes you great.

The world's party throws you in the sewer.

God's party gives you authority and restores your inheritance.

The world's party strips you naked and humiliates you.

Now, I know there are many of you readers who consider the younger son's actions, or even my actions as a teenager, and you can't relate. You've lived a pretty clean life. Well, I think the God of extravagant parties has something to say to you as well. Let's pick things up at the last part of the parable.

"Meanwhile, the older son was in the field. When he came near the house, he heard music and dancing. So he called one of the servants and asked him what was going on. 'Your brother has come,' he replied, 'and your father has killed the fattened calf because he has him back safe and sound.' The older brother became angry and refused to go in. So his father went out and pleaded with him. But he answered his father, 'Look! All these years I've been slaving for you and never disobeyed your orders. Yet you never gave me even a young goat so I could celebrate with my friends. But when this son of yours who has squandered your property with prostitutes comes home, you kill the fattened calf for him!' 'My son,' the father said, 'you are always with me, and everything I have is yours. But we had to celebrate and be glad, because this brother of yours was dead and is alive again; he was lost and is found.'"
- Luke 15:25-32

For those of you who have lived your life following God without running to a far off country, do you still think life is about what you can earn? That if you work hard enough you just might be able to squeak by? I want to tell you, that's not the Father's heart.

My kids live in a nice house because their dad lives in a nice house. My kids have surfboards not because they worked for them and saved up over months and years. No, they surf because their dad gave them surfboards. My kids get to go on vacations not because they've been mowing lawns since they were four years old, but because I take care of them ... because I'm their dad and love to lavish them with the best.

That's how God is. He says to us, "Everything I have is yours."
I challenge you to meditate on this: God is not stingy.
We ask for a little goat ... God gives us a cow! We ask for a
sliver of beef jerky ... God gives us a veal cutlet! The fact is that
when the younger son returned, the father said he had to celebrate. He couldn't help himself. The same goes with God. He
cannot turn a passive eye when we turn to Him. He doesn't look
glumly from heaven and doubt our sincerity. He lavishes us with
blessing! He shouts His elation for all to hear. There are a lot of
things in life that we have to do. We have to go to school. We
have to pay our taxes. We have to floss (though most of us don't).
What is it that God says He has to do?

He has to celebrate.

Our God is a partying God.

It says in Luke 15 that whenever someone comes home,
there's a literal party going on in heaven. Can't you just see it? The
angels going crazy, throwing golden confetti all over the place,
blasting their harp music while God dances around in the center
of it all shouting, "My boy's come home ... my girl's come back!"
He is the King of celebration.

Some of you have never felt celebrated over. You've never
had people single you out to say how glad they are that you're on
the earth. Maybe you've never even had a birthday party. Well,
let me tell you that when you give your life to Jesus, all of heaven
stops in your honor and throws a party. I'm serious. It might
sound like a fairy tale. But it's in the Bible, which is to say, it's
true. When you turn to God, heaven throws a party, and you're
the centerpiece.

Our God is a God who celebrates.

And He wants to celebrate you.

It starts with your simple acceptance that He is who He
says He is and He'll do what He said He'll do. He can take your

messed up life, no matter how far you've run or how low you've fallen. You might think yourself so far gone you're beyond hope. But nothing could be further from the truth. He loves you. He's waiting for you. And He'll run to you and scoop you up in His arms before you even know what's going on.

Give Him a chance.

I dare you.

Party on.

2

CALLED TO PARTY

A while back I was walking on the beach in San Diego where I live, when I noticed in the distance the warm glow of hanging lights. Curious, I drew near in the fading dusk and realized it was a party at the Hotel Del Coronado.

Now if you don't know about this hotel, just imagine the grandest, most elaborate haven of all things awesome, and you'll come pretty close. Not only is it one of the most expensive places to stay in the world, but it's quite possibly one of the grandest locations to spend an evening anywhere.

So, I wasn't surprised when I walked up to behold a party of Great Gatsby proportions. Beneath the hanging lights were long white draped tables adorned with a veritable feast: grilled fish, prime rib, lobster, crab, and such an assortment of side dishes as to make my head spin. And the desserts! I'd never seen such a display. Suffice it to say, I was beholding a masterpiece of celebratory splendor. Men and women moseyed about in suits and sundresses, umbrellas in their drinks, chatting and laughing giddily without a care in the world.

I admit, I felt a stab of envy.

Would have been nice to be part of the party.

Not long after, as I strolled along the same beach, I beheld a sight of stark contrast. With San Diego serving as host to a naval base, it wasn't uncommon to see military personnel here and there throughout the city. There on the beach I saw a group of soldiers in utter misery. They were in their full fatigues, hats, and combat boots, but instead of jogging over the sand in tight rows like you see in the movies, these guys were two feet out into the water, sitting down. It being the middle of winter, the water was frigid and crashed over their shoulders in icy waves that made me shiver just looking at them.

As if this wasn't enough, a drill sergeant circled about them, screaming in their faces as loud as he could. At his signal, they all leaned back to do an underwater sit up. Some of them toppled sideways in the current, immediately drawing fiery wrath from the drill instructor. Over and over again they dipped down and rose up, choking and gasping as the Pacific waters tried to swallow them whole.

I stood watching them from afar—feet sunk into cool sand, clothes perfectly dry, and thought to myself, *I have never been so thankful to be free in my life. Thank you Jesus!*

As I walked off, leaving the soldiers behind, I began to ponder a sad reality: Most of the world equates Christianity with the soldiers in the water.

"Why in the world would I ever become a Christian?" they muse. "Most of the ones I know look like they've been sucking on lemons." They assume God is like the mean drill sergeant, spewing constant disapproval as he pummels us into miserable submission.

Sometimes Christians don't help the matter. Oh, how we complain about how bad things are and how sinful everyone is! They hear us talking about wrath and punishment, and render

Jesus about as attractive as a gas station bathroom.

But listen carefully here ... the Bible says that's it's His kindness that brings us to repentance.

The world is dying to see joyful Christians.

Every soul on the planet, whether they know it or not, longs to see the God of celebration and joy and love. They want to know the Jesus that forgives. The one who draws them not with scorn or shame, but with kindness, with mercy, and with love. Deep down, we're all like the woman caught in adultery in the Bible, thrown at Jesus' feet by those who wished to condemn her. Jesus knelt by her side and accepted her without a shred of judgment. He forgave her sins and told her to go and sin no more. Every human heart craves this kind of acceptance, this kind of grace. In a world so bereft of warmth, people hunger for closeness, for belonging. And there is no belonging comparable to that offered by Jesus. Not even close.

He invites all to His Kingdom party.

But how many of us listen, and come running?

The Kingdom of God is a great big celebration. It's all over the Bible. It's why we throw Baptism bashes at our church here in San Diego because they are the ultimate celebration of God's redemptive hand in our lives. We invite everyone to a huge picnic with tons of free food and games and music. Folks throwing the ball around. People wolfing down fried chicken and potato salad. Everyone clapping like crazy when, one by one, folks walked down into the Pacific waters to be dunked for glory. Everyone cheering. Everyone having the time of their life.

Baptisms should be like really good birthday parties. There should be laughing and singing and feasting. Your friends should be there. Your family should be there. What better reason is there to celebrate than a life given to God? Is this a time to be somber? To sit all stoic in a pew and clap a golf clap or mumble an "amen" when the believer rises from the water? No! It's a time to cut loose!

That's also why our main outreach every year is our Halloween harvest fest. We take a night—a night usually dedicated to the celebration of evil—and turn it on its slimy little head by throwing a God party. We invite everyone we can, welcome them where it's safe and clean and fun, and we tell them they're loved by us, and by God.

Now some of you might be thinking I'm a little over the top. Of course he thinks this way, you reason. *He's a pastor. It's his job to make people get excited about God.* And some of you might be thinking I'm forging my own theology that has little to do with the Bible. Well, don't just take my word for it. Let's look at the Bible.

Look at these verses in Exodus, where God actually commands His people to celebrate.

"This is a day you are to commemorate; for the generations to come you shall celebrate it as a festival to the LORD—a lasting ordinance."
- Exodus 12:14

So many of us view the Old Testament as a stuffy collection of outdated laws. We usually skip over entire sections of text when it just seems like God is telling us all kinds of things to do. But if you really read it, you will find over and over again, a call to party.

"Three times a year you are to celebrate a festival to me."
- Exodus 23:14

"Celebrate the festival of the harvest with the first fruits of the crops you sow in your fields. Celebrate the festival of ingathering at

the end of the year when you gather your crops from the fields."
- Exodus 23:16

Are you convinced yet that God wants us to celebrate?

Well, in case you're not fully convinced ... if you're still like, *Yeah ... well, Robert, maybe so, but I feel like you're just pulling out some extraneous verses to prove a point.*

To that, I say ... look at this other verse that will positively blow your mind.

"'So beginning with the fifteenth day of the seventh month, after you have gathered the crops of the land, celebrate the festival to the LORD for seven days; the first day is a day of sabbath rest, and the eighth day also is a day of sabbath rest."
- Leviticus 23:39

Wow. We think a party is pretty long if it goes for three or four hours, right? Now imagine a party lasting all day. Okay. Now multiply that by seven. That's a WEEK LONG PARTY! I don't know about you, but I can feel myself getting fatter just thinking about it. Seven days of fun. Seven days of feasting. Seven days of celebration. Unbelievable. Picture yourself going into your boss's office with this kind of request.

"Hey, I need to take a week off of work," you ask.

He (or she) looks up from a massive oak desk. "You going on vacation?"

"No," you say. "I'm throwing a party. A seven day party."

An entire week for jollification? What a waste of time and money. You could devote yourself to much greater pursuits than frittering away your resources at the altar of enjoyment.

But God took celebration seriously. So seriously, in fact, that he allotted an entire day *after the party* for rest. He wanted to

25

make sure we were refreshed and ready to get back to work after partying so hard. Good grief, is this really in the Bible?

Some of you reading this book are sinning big time.

What's the crime, you ask?

Not partying enough!

Go to your family and friends, knock on their doors, and thrust a forceful finger in their faces. "Sinners!" you can say. "You're not serious about following the Lord, are you?"

"What?" they look back at you, perplexed. "What are you talking about?"

"You're not partying enough! Time to chill out and have some fun."

Then you bust out the fajitas and piñatas.

Don't you think more people would be coming to God if they knew this was how we were supposed to act? All those folks who scowl at the mere mention of church, declaring they would never darken its door because they think God is harsh and hard and out to ruin their lives. If they only knew the truth!

God has this against his people: we don't party enough.

For a while now I've tried to apply this to my life, and my family's life. One of the core values of the Herber clan is to be good partiers. So how does this work out? Well, when I hear that a party is going on and my family is invited, we're going to go. Period. We don't just consider the invitation as take it or leave it. No way. We're going to be the first ones there, smiling ear to ear. If it's a costume party, we're going to be decked out in whatever theme is called for. Cowboy party? You better believe we'll have our hats and bandanas. If it's a Hawaiian luau party … you know we'll be wearing leis and floral shirts and straw hats with smears of sunscreen on our noses. We are not to be outdone. Not because we're competitive. We're just all-in kind of people.

When there's great food at a party, I'm not all pastor-like and letting everyone else enjoy the grub as I eat a cracker in a corner. NO! I'm diving toward those tables and piling my plate with every last succulent offering. I'm going to taste and see that the Lord's hors d'oeruves are GOOD! Did God give me this tongue with all these taste buds for no reason? I think not.

When there's dancing, mark my words, I am not going to let some group of spastic college students steal my thunder. I'm the partying pastor. I'm gonna get out there with my smokin' hot wife, and all four of my kids along for the ride.

If you've ever been to a party with us, you're sure to have seen the Herbers jamming down on the dance floor. Even my little five-year-old tries to bust a move. It's awesome. And why shouldn't it be?

Here's the difference: In a holy party, people build each other up instead of tear each other down. In a holy party, people celebrate each other instead of scamming on each other. You don't have to walk around all insecure about what people think about you, what you look like, or anything at all besides enjoying God and God's people.

As a dad, the only responsible thing I can do as the leader of my family is to be a great role model in the area of partying. I want to teach my kids how to party! I want them to know what it's like to party with Jesus. You know why? I don't want the world teaching them its cheap, dark, destructive party methods. It's not my place to scowl with my arms crossed and always say, "No, no, no!" all the time. My place is to show them how awesome it is to walk with Jesus—to model for them the joy of celebrating God. That way, they don't look at the world and pine for what they're missing. They don't see the slime and the shadows and think it looks like fun. No! They think their dad is fun! God's party ain't a creaky pew and a boring sermon—it's the greatest party the world has ever known. The greatest joy of the human heart.

While the world's party always leaves us empty and dead inside ... God's party fills us with life. It's what we were made for. I honestly believe it's what heaven is all about. A great, big, eternal party for the glory and presence of God. So when my kids see me smiling from ear to ear, dancing smack dab in the middle of the dance floor, they know why I do it. And, by God's grace, they dance right alongside me.

Are you too deliberate to party? Or do you assume such a thing isn't your personality? That's fair. Not everyone is wired the same. But let me just nudge you a little to break out of that shell and stretch your party wings. Why? Because God wants you to do it. Why? So that you would revere his name. Why? So that you would remember how good He has been to you. It's about enjoying the good things the Lord has given to His people.

Let's look at another verse that really pushes the edge on our common perceptions.

"Be sure to set aside a tenth of all that your fields produce each year. Eat the tithe of your grain, new wine and olive oil, and the firstborn of your herds and flocks in the presence of the LORD your God at the place he will choose as a dwelling for his Name, so that you may learn to revere the LORD your God always."
- Deuteronomy 14:22-23

God is saying this: *I want you to have a feast so that you can remember to revere me.*

When I'm studying these scriptures and discovering new truths, whenever possible I try to put them into practice in my life. The staff here at All Peoples Church starts every week the same. We come together at 8:30 on Monday mornings and have a staff meeting. Usually what it looks like is some worship, some prayer, then I'll share a little message from what God is speaking to me that week. We'll discuss our strategy, divvy up the work, then roll up our sleeves and dive in.

A while back I was spending time with the Lord before we had our typical staff meeting and I felt His leading to do something different. To shake things up a bit. I called one of my assistant pastors on the phone and told him we weren't having a normal staff meeting that day.

"What do you want to do?" he asked.

"Let's meet at Santana's."

"Understood."

And indeed he did. For Santana's is one of the most glorious locations in all of San Diego, serving up quite possibly the most glorious culinary miracle in all of God's creation: the breakfast burrito.

Soon afterwards, our entire staff gathered round a table at the restaurant, complimentary burritos steaming before us all. I told them why we were there.

"Guys, you know the verse we've been studying about how God had to celebrate. Well, that's why we're here. The past few weeks have been a challenge for all of us. We've fasted and prayed and worked our tails off, but the fruit has been our very first two-service Sunday. Way to go!"

Everyone beamed and nodded as they stuffed copious amounts of burrito into their mouths. "Guys, we have over a hundred people volunteering on Sundays for the church. That's incredible!"

Another person chimed in. "I'm pumped, we're seeing so much joy rise up in people's hearts. I've really noticed it since we've been studying about The Partying God."

"We're seeing more salvations than ever!" someone added.

A final statement blew our minds: "We started this church years ago with zero people and last week we had over eight hundred and forty attend."

With every declaration our joy level lifted.

Eventually we went around the table and expressed different ways we were personally encouraged. As each person shared, I was reminded how important it is to recall the goodness of God. As humans we are so forgetful. How often are our blessings overshadowed by challenges or frustrations? Soon the whole world grows dark and our lives become tinted with difficulty. But when we remember and declare those things that God has done, light creeps back in and joy arises.

The last order of business for our holy burrito bash was an encouragement time for a girl on staff named Sierra. She'd been working at the church for years, but it had always been her dream to go overseas as a missionary. For a long time she thought her dream had died because of certain challenges, but that very week we were about to send her out and fulfill her dream. As a kind of going away present every person at the table told Sierra what she meant to them, what they saw in her, and what they felt her destiny would hold. Do you think Sierra was encouraged? Of course she was! But not just her. All of us were brimming with joy.

Sometimes you just have to press pause and celebrate. There's always more work to do. There's always constructive criticism that we can bring. But the heart of God is that we stop at times and throw a party, be it large or small. For when we celebrate, we remember to honor God.

Let's continue unpacking Deuteronomy 14. Trust me ... you want to read on.

"But if the place is too distant and you've been blessed by the

LORD *your God and cannot carry your tithes because the place where the* LORD *will choose to carry His name is too far then exchange your tithe for silver and take the silver with you and go to the place the* LORD *your God will choose. Use the silver to buy whatever you like. Cattle, sheep, wine, or other fermented drink or anything you wish, then you and your household shall eat there in the presence of the* LORD *your God and rejoice."*
- *Deuteronomy 14:24-26*

Okay. Wait a second here. Stop everything you're doing (besides reading this book of course) and think about what you just read. This is about tithing. You know, the whole pass-the-bucket-and-drop-your-dough-in idea? Church funds come from tithes. It's how we have buildings and staff and practical outreach to the community. God's Word instructs us to tithe.

In his book *The Kingdom of God is a Party,* Tony Campolo says that this passage points out that in certain situations, we are to use our tithe to buy *whatever* we want. Even wine, people! Now, growing up as a teetotaling Christian ... I admit, this is challenging. But there's no denying its presence. Another translation says we are to buy "whatever our appetite craves" then eat before the Lord and rejoice. Where did we get the idea that acceptable worship only involves painful sacrifice and rejecting every personal need? According to this verse, the opposite seems true.

Let me break it down ever simpler. From my perspective, God is saying that in certain situations, we are to put aside a percentage of your income to buy whatever you wish so you can party. Hello?

Have you seen this before? If your thing is beef tenderloin, then buy some cows. If you love lamb gyros, then buy the lamb. If you're vegan, then buy all the tofu you've ever dreamed of. God wants us to sit down together and eat in His presence and rejoice.

The Lord is serious about us learning to party.

I'm not sure you believe me yet.

A lot of us have a hard time with this truth because our parents weren't deliberate about celebrating. Children take the cues from their moms and dads automatically. Maybe your parents said life was all about hard work, or maybe they were lazy, or maybe you didn't have parents who lived in your household at all. We all grew up programmed by our family life to some extent, for good or ill.

My parents were very deliberate about celebrating. I count myself immensely blessed. We didn't have a bunch of money growing up, but my mom would always invest in decorations for the house. Any holiday that came around, the house would transform. At Thanksgiving she'd have all these decorative turkeys set out everywhere along with fall flowers and pumpkins. But it wasn't just decorations. It was music. I still remember that record player where Mom would put on albums at Christmas, most commonly, *Chipmunks Christmas*. To this day, years and years later, I start craving chipmunk tunes come December.

I remember being off at college and yearning to come home just for the celebrations. The meals. The warmth. The welcome. Of course, what food could have compared to Mom's chili con queso, fresh salsa, guacamole, and tamales so good you want to tango.

God wants us to live a life of celebration. To keep our eyes open to ways we can delight in His goodness. Let me give you three reasons why.

First, God is a loving Father and He loves to party with His children.

Let me tell you, as a father of four, there is no better time of day than when I sit down at the head of the table for dinner and my kids are all gathered around me. Listening to them tell stories and celebrating victories together—not to mention eating my wife's delectable creations—makes dinnertime the apex of my schedule. Just being with them fills my heart with love as we recall the good things God has done.

Second, parties create community.

In the modern world we live very disconnected lives. Walk into any coffee shop, a place you would think would foster connection, and everyone has their little iPhone and ear buds, completely cut off from one another. We drive into our garages, the door slides down, then we hide out behind our privacy fences cooking BBQ without the slightest thought of inviting the next door neighbor. It's like we live these parallel lives in plastic bubbles, never touching, never talking, just rolling along in our lonely little worlds.

But parties bring us together.

Acts 2:46 says this, *"Everyday they were meeting together in the temple courts. They broke bread in their homes and ate together with glad and sincere hearts."*

The early church knew how to party.

There are few things that break down walls and bring people together like sharing a meal. If your church has small groups that meet together, I encourage you to join one. And then bring some guacamole and chips. You'll become an instant celebrity.

Lastly, parties draw people in.

I'm reminded of a story told on YouTube by pastor Tony Campolo. He was visiting Honolulu, Hawaii on a ministry trip a few years back and found himself wide awake in the middle of the night, his stomach rumbling with hunger. He decided to set out in search of a restaurant. The only place still open at that hour was a run down little diner up a side street with no booths, just a countertop and a row of rundown stools.

He took a seat, noticed a greasy spoon on the countertop

and looked up as the rotund diner owner in a dirty white apron walked out of the kitchen, plucked a cigar out of his mouth and asked him what he wanted to eat.

"A cup of coffee and a donut."

The guy nodded, poured coffee into a cup, then wiped his hands on his soiled shirt before grabbing a donut from behind a glass case and serving it up on a plate. Tony watched the owner return the cigar to his mouth and trudge away to the kitchen. He began drinking his coffee and eating his dirty donut at three-thirty in the morning, when suddenly a loud group of women flung open the door and herded into the diner. Tony counted eight or nine prostitutes as they hopped into the stools on either side of him, clutching the dirty menus in search of something to eat. Beet red embarrassed, Tony kept his head down and tried to disappear.

And then the lady on his right opened up her mouth and spoke loud enough for everyone to hear. "Tomorrow's my birthday. I'm gonna be thirty-nine."

No sooner had she said this than the woman to Tony's left piped up in a mocking voice, "So what do you want? A birthday cake? You want us to throw you a party or something?"

The first woman dropped her gaze to the countertop and shook her head. "Why do you have to put me down like that?" And then, with a crack in her voice she said, "I've never had a birthday party in my life. I don't expect one *now*."

Tony kept his eyes forward. He couldn't help but be riveted by what he'd just heard. He waited for the prostitutes to finish their meal and leave before he called the owner over.

"Yeah, what do ya want?" the owner barked.

"Do those women come here every night?"

"Yeah, sure."

"And the one sitting next to me?" Tony motioned toward his right.

"You mean Agnes," he said.

Tony paused a moment as a thin smile spread across his face. "Tomorrow's her birthday. What do you say we decorate the place and when she comes in tomorrow we throw a birthday party for her. She's never had a birthday party her whole life."

The diner owner leaned forward, pointed his beefy finger right at Tony's face. "Mister, that's brilliant!" Then he turned toward the kitchen and shouted, "Jane! This guy wants to throw a birthday party for Agnes."

A few seconds later the guy's wife appeared, wide-eyed with disbelief. She leaned toward Tony and took his hand. "Mister," she said. "You wouldn't understand this because of what she does, you know, as a job. But that woman is one of the kindest people in this town."

"Well, then can I decorate the place?" Tony asked.

"To your heart's content," she said.

"And I'll bring a birthday cake."

Harry the diner owner shook his head and barked, "No no … the cake is my thing!"

They finished up their plan and Tony bid them goodnight. The next morning he made a Kmart run for crêpe paper and streamers, balloons and poster board. Just a few hours later he returned to the diner and worked until the once grimy establishment was transformed. He made a big sign that said "Happy Birthday, Agnes" and taped it to the mirror behind the counter. He strung streamers from one wall to the other and blew up balloons. The diner had never looked so good.

Jane, the owner's wife who did all the cooking, got the word out on the street so that by 3:15 in the morning every prostitute in Honolulu had crammed into the place. It was wall-to-wall prostitutes. At 3:30 the door opened. In walked Agnes and her friends. Right at that moment a hundred voices shouted, "Happy birthday, Agnes!"

Tony had never seen anyone so stunned in his life. Her knees buckled, she swayed on her feet and those nearby had to lead her to a seat. The birthday song erupted, and by the time they sang "Happy birthday, dear Agnes … " the cake was brought out, glowing with candles.

It was then that she began to cry.

Harry stood there awkwardly with the cake in his arms as she wept, until finally he'd had enough.

"All right, Agnes … knock it off and blow out the candles."

She gathered herself enough to lean forward and attempt to blow out the flames, but couldn't manage in her emotional state. Finally, Harry gave up and blew out the candles on her behalf. He handed her a knife. "Now cut the cake, Agnes … come on now."

She sat there for a long while, knife in hand, then looked over at Tony. "Is it okay if I don't cut the cake? What I'd really like to do is take the cake home and show it to my mother."

"It's your cake," he said.

She nodded, stood up, and picked the cake up in her arms.

"Do you have to do it now?" he asked.

"I just live two doors down," she assured him. "Let me take the cake home. I'll be right back, I promise."

With her precious cargo Agnes pushed through the crowd, and out the door into the sultry Hawaiian night. As the door slowly swung shut, there was dead silence. The whole group was stunned. After a few uneasy moments, Tony spoke up.

"What do you say we pray?"

Everyone stared back at him in shock.

His prayer began as a cry of freedom. "God, I pray you would deliver her from what dirty rotten men have done to her, her whole life. I pray you would make her new. That you would bring back everything that's been taken from her. Amen."

When Tony opened his eyes, Harry was right in his face. "Hey Compolo! You didn't tell me you were a preacher," he grumbled. "What kind of church you belong to?"

And right then, as if God had given him the perfect words to say, Tony answered. "I belong to a church that throws birthday parties for whores at 3:30 in the morning."

Harry looked him straight in the eyes, unconvinced. "No you don't," he said. "No you don't! If there was a church like that, I'd be a part of it."

Wouldn't we all? Tony thought to himself.

What if we as Christians threw parties for people who no one else cared about? What if the body of Christ became known as the people who loved those who had never been loved? I think a church like that would be irresistible. I think people could hardly stay away from God if that happened.

What are we waiting for?

3

JESUS LOVES PARTIES

When I was a senior in college I was just beginning to comprehend my role in inviting people into the Kingdom of God. I'd experienced such personal change over recent years, it only made sense for me to begin 'casting the net,' so to speak. My first efforts took place in a lecture hall during a class called Neuroscience. I remember sitting there in my seat eyeing the various students sitting nearby, wondering how to segue naturally into the Gospel. In the end, I settled on the most logical approach.

Considering the fact that I always studied better in groups, I initiated with several folks sitting nearby and asked if they wanted to get together soon to study for the upcoming exam. A guy and a girl said yes and that night we gathered round a table at the library, quizzing each other on the mysteries of the human brain. At the end of the session I turned to the girl and asked her a question.

"Have you ever read the Bible?"

She was a rather gloomy person and seemed altogether unimpressed with life. I'd learned that she was living with her boyfriend at the time and was certainly far from God. Asking her

39

about the Bible seemed non-threatening enough, and might give me an "in" if it piqued her curiosity.

She looked back at me and shook her head. "No."

"Well, do you have a Bible?"

Again, the answer was no.

"I'd love to give you one if you want."

"Yeah, of course," she said casually.

A little later I set out for the bookstore and bought her a copy of *The Message*, a modern, conversational paraphrase of the Bible. I assumed it would be the easiest for her to read since she'd never been exposed to scripture before. As I handed her the Bible I made one request.

"Would you mind doing me a favor? How about you read the first three chapters of the book of John and then let me know what you think."

Little did she know I was setting up a Holy Spirit ambush. I imagined her reading through those first three chapters, digesting one of the richest theological treatises ever written, starting off with Jesus revealed as the Son of God, and finishing off with possibly the most well-known verse in Bible: *"For God so loved the world that He gave His one and only son …"*

She'd read, be struck to the core, and give her life to Jesus right then and there. It was a perfect set up!

She took the book gladly, and bid me goodbye. Every day I prayed that as she read those verses she'd be touched. When the next study session finally arrived I was eager to hear what she thought about the Bible.

Trying not to sound too excited I brought up my request "So," I said in faux nonchalance, "Did you have a chance to, you know, read that book I gave you? Maybe the first three chapters or something?"

She smiled suddenly, eyes brightening. "Yeah, I did!"

Oh my goodness! I thought. *This is it.*

"So, what did you think about what you read?"

I'll never forget what she said.

"I never knew that Jesus partied! And with his mom!"

Her words were like a swift punch to the gut. *What?* Is that all she got out of it? Are you kidding me? This is the Son of God we're talking about. You know, savior of the world and all? How could she make such a sacrilegious observation? I mean here we have one of the most beautiful theological statements in all of scripture ... *In the beginning was the Word and the Word was with God and the Word was God* ... and all she got was 'Jesus partied with his mom'? Unbelievable.

I walked off, trying my best to hide any disappointment, but the opportunity seemed wholly wasted. Then after a few minutes, as I mulled over the conversation on the way home, it hit me.

That was brilliant.

Jesus did it again, I thought. *He broke into someone's irreligious life and made himself understandable.* That girl was totally unchurched and had no interest whatsoever in a sterile observation of rules and rituals. But she read this part of the Bible and she suddenly connected with Jesus for the first time because he went to a party, just like her! She was intrigued. Not by churchy people, but by a real, loving, spontaneous, unpredictable, compassionate, all powerful God, who humbled himself and became a man ... Jesus. A man who liked to have a good time with his followers. For the first time in her life she was confronted with truth, and from a most unexpected angle.

The more I thought about it, the more my entire evangelistic paradigm was turned on its head. If Jesus was drawing this girl in through a party, maybe I should change my strategy? So the next week at class I extended an invitation.

"Hey Sarah," I said. "I want to invite you to a kind of dinner party with some friends of mine. We call it Lifegroup. And every week we get together and eat a bunch of food and play games. Then we just open the Bible and talk about what it means. You want to come?"

I admit, I doubted she'd say yes, but at least it was worth a try.

"Yeah! I'd love to," she said, visibly excited.

My eyebrows shot up with surprise. "Really? That's great."

I gave her the time and place and left class that day more charged than ever. We started praying as a Lifegroup, that she'd come to know God's love in a powerful way. And when she finally came a couple days later, I was amazed by how easily she fit in, smiling and laughing and genuinely taking part. At the end of the night, Sarah actually gave her life to Jesus.

All because of a party.

I learned that day that Jesus doesn't wait for us to break into His world. Rather, He breaks into ours. He meets us where we are and settles down before us, eye to eye. The more I read the Bible the more I realize how much time Jesus spent going to parties. If you look at the book of Luke it seems He's practically eating His way through that Gospel, just going from one dinner to another, one feast to the next.

Here's what I've realized: Jesus used parties as a kind of missional strategy.

Jesus calls Matthew, one of His disciples, and immediately they have a party. Jesus chooses a party as the setting of His first miracle—the wedding at Cana. Jesus goes to some friends' house (remember Lazarus, Mary, and Martha?) and He ends up having a dinner party. He goes to the Feast of the Tabernacle, the Passover feast, the Feast of Dedication. Then we see Jesus talking in parables, and so often the setting of the story is a party. By mere observation we can easily deduce that Jesus used parties and celebrations and festivals as tools to advance His Kingdom. That's the whole reason I'm writing this book.

Just the other day I had a gentleman share with me how much studying this aspect of Jesus' life has helped him understand God's heart of blessing and celebration. We could all use this realization. Our natural tendency is to strive and labor for the things of God in an attempt to earn His favor. We read the Bible like a notch in the belt, we pray like earning a badge. We do things for the sake of doing them as if the mere action was the point. But Jesus came to earth to cut right through our human efforts to reach God. If we realized this, churches would be a much happier place. And in turn, so would the world.

So let's jump into the Bible (i.e. Your Party Manual) and see what more God has to say on the subject. The passage I want to unpack is in Luke 19 and takes place in the ancient city of Jericho.

First, let's lay down some historical background.

This city was not that great of a place. It had actually been destroyed in the Old Testament for its immorality. (Check out the book of Joshua for this account. It's pretty epic.) And in fact when it was reestablished in the New Testament it was done so by Herod the Great, a tyrannical king, Jewish in name only. Simply put, the guy was a very rough character. Jericho was much more akin to Las Vegas than anything else, rather than a spiritual city like Jerusalem (where Jews routinely took pilgrimages). It's likely that much of the population warned folks away from visiting Jericho, citing its rampant carnality and wild culture. No self-respecting Jew would be caught dead visiting such a place.

But Jesus didn't seem to care.

We find Him walking right into the middle of this infamous city. Why? I believe He simply wanted to show people the love of the Father. Jesus seems motivated by this time and time again, going to the places where people lived and worked who might not otherwise hear a word about God or salvation. Places where religious people wouldn't be caught dead.

"Jesus entered Jericho and was passing through. A man was there by the name of Zacchaeus; he was a chief tax collector and was wealthy. He wanted to see who Jesus was, but because he was short he could not see over the crowd. So he ran ahead and climbed a sycamore-fig tree to see him, since Jesus was coming that way."
- *Luke 19:1-4*

Let us consider something here before moving on. From a socially Jewish standpoint, Zacchaeus was a total reject. Collecting taxes for the Romans, an occupying, tyrannical force, was synonymous with treason. Imagine a Frenchman collecting taxes for the Nazis during World War II, bleeding his country-men dry for the sake of personal gain. One can easily see why such a man would not be popular in any way, shape, or form. Who knows why "Zacch" chose such a sordid career path. Maybe he'd been called "shorty" one too many times by the locals and joined the Romans as a kind of revenge. We'll never know. Either way, the guy was not well liked. Okay, back to the story.

"When Jesus reached the spot, He looked up and said to him, 'Zacchaeus, come down immediately. I must stay at your house today.' So he came down at once and welcomed him gladly."
- *Luke 19:5-6*

Let's paint this picture: A super star celebrity walks down the road, famous for healing and bread-multiplying and walking on water and calming storms.

The crowd presses in to catch a glimpse of the guy as He passes by. When Jesus looks up and sees the short guy in the tree,

He stops in His tracks and calls out the town reject by name. Everyone within earshot must have gasped. I imagine folks standing in shocked silence as Jesus invites Himself to Zacch's house. The chief tax collector? That spineless worm traitor? This can't be right.

But Jesus saw the guy's hunger and singled him out. Now, what's really interesting to me here is that Jesus didn't say, 'Yo, Zacchaeus! Come down so we can go to church!' or 'Come down so we can visit the temple together and present sacrifices!' or 'Let's go to a prayer meeting!'

Not at all.

He said, "Zacch, I'm coming to your house today."

All eyes upon him, shorty scrambles down the tree in utter disbelief. He gleefully leads the way to his posh apartment on the ritzy side of town where he promptly throws a dinner party. Without an ounce of hesitation Zacchaeus welcomes Jesus in with joy, because Jesus had paid him special regard. He had given him honor, though no honor was due.

But there were other things going on at the same time. As the loser/traitor/tax collector led the prophet and His gang away to his house, the people grumbled. "He has gone to be the guest of a notorious sinner," they said. Was Jesus blind? Did He not realize who it was He was hanging with? I'm sure more than a few folks went home with an anti-Jesus stance that day. They were probably upstanding citizens who considered themselves far more worthy to fellowship with Jesus.

Several years ago I did a teaching series about sharing the love of Jesus with those who don't yet know Him. I talked about the need to go to the places where these people could be found, instead of waiting for them to come to us. This might mean going to parties. Maybe even bars or clubs. After one of these sermons an older gentlemen walked up, apparently a bit disturbed.

"You know, I don't think this is a good message for you to preach," he said. "Haven't you heard the adage that bad company corrupts good morals? We need to teach our folks to stay far away from those kinds of people."

I tried my best to smile and listen well, but when he finished I said. "I see where you're coming from. But when I read the Bible, that's not what Jesus did. He went into the midst of the party because He knew that He would influence them, not the other way around."

During the season I preached this sermon series, I was living in Texas, working at a church in Waco's inner-city. We had moved into a run-down neighborhood where we could more easily reach out to those around us. I really wanted to shine the light of Christ, though I was still a bit uncertain about exactly how to do it in such a setting.

But within days I met a gentleman who lived across the street named Cenobio Banda. We struck up an unlikely friendship, talking every few days as neighbors do. Every so often he'd throw these parties in his front yard, Tejano music blaring, fragrant smoke wafting in all directions as they grilled up all sorts of mouth watering Mexican grub. I'd wave from my front porch and he'd always respond with a wave back and a big smile.

One day, to my surprise, he invited me to one of his parties. But this time, it wasn't in his yard; this time it was going be really big in a nearby venue.

"Oh Robert, you gotta come. There's gonna be food and drinks and music. You'll love it."

I knew we'd probably be the only Christians there, not to mention the only gringos, but I wasn't going to pass it up.

Days later my wife and I walked into that huge hall he'd rented. It was chock full of strangers, Latino music pounding the air, copious decorations hanging from the walls and tables. I felt altogether out of place.

Until I heard a booming voice from across the room.

"Hey Robert!"

It was Cenobio, smiling wide, motioning for us to join him at the head table. We made our way through the crowd, feeling awkward but welcomed. He sat us down at the table and, beaming with pride, started introducing me one by one to the folks in the room. There were at least a hundred people there.

"Hey, this here's my friend Robert," he'd say over and over again, leading me to person after person to shake my hand. Later on I asked him how many people at the party were in his family.

"Oh," he chuckled. "This is all my family ... actually, this here's only a part of my family."

As the night wore on, I realized that simply showing up to his party made him feel valued. He felt loved because I had jumped into his world. And you know what? Just two weeks later he came over to my house with his two sons and a son-in-law and right there in my study, they all gave their lives to Jesus. And it didn't stop there. Within the next six months, fifteen members of his family came to Christ.

Why?

Because Jesus wants us to step into other people's worlds. He wants to show people a glimpse of his own party, the only one that truly satisfies.

I'm not talking about straddling the fence in a two-faced duality, with one foot in the world indulging in the flesh, and the other foot walking with God. I'm talking about ushering the Kingdom into dark places. Places desperate for hope. I'm talking about going in with a vision and a mission to tell others about God's party.

This is what Jesus was doing.

"But Zacchaeus stood up and said to the Lord, 'Look, Lord! Here and now I give half of my possessions to the poor, and if I have cheated anybody out of anything, I will pay back four times the amount.'"
- *Luke 19:8*

While the religious crowd still mocked and criticized Jesus' choice of friends, this guy Zacch decided in the middle of a party to turn his life around and live for others' good. Think about it. Music pumping, food aplenty, and he looks Jesus right in the eyes and declares his radical new intentions. Jesus didn't tell him to do it. He didn't sit at the edge of the room, stiff with discomfort, arms folded over His chest, with a stern look of disapproval on His face. No, I imagine Him smiling wide, listening to His new friend's life story, maybe even swaying to the music here and there and sipping the prize wine that Zacchaeus surely brought out for such an occasion.

Jesus wasn't embarrassed. Zacch wasn't ridiculed. He was simply accepted with joy. How I wish I could have been there to see the expression on Jesus' face right at that moment when the tax collector's heart melted into something beautiful.

When people encounter Jesus in an authentic way He starts transforming them from the inside out. When we tell people about Jesus, we're not inviting people into a religious system of rules. We're inviting them to a relationship with a real person ... to someone who can transform them to the very core.

Without a sermon preached or even an altar call, Zacch lays it all down for Jesus. He realizes he's a sinner and vows to change. By the mere presence of the Savior, this guy was transformed.

Listen to what Jesus says next.

"Jesus said to him, 'Today salvation has come to this house, because this man, too, is a son of Abraham. For the Son of Man came to seek and to save the lost.'"
- Luke 19:9-10

Why does Jesus love to go to parties? Because that's where He finds the lost and the hurting. And He came not just for the righteous, but to reach out to those in desperate need. I believe He is commissioning us today, here and now, to get into the world of the hurting and the broken and the lost all around us.

If this is not exciting to you, please check your pulse.

There's nothing greater.

Let's visit another passage of scripture to explore how Jesus used this principle.

"As Jesus went on from there, he saw a man named Matthew sitting at the tax collector's booth. 'Follow me,' he told him, and Matthew got up and followed him."
- Matthew 9:9

Here we have another tax collector that Jesus singles out, going right up to his table and telling the guy to give it all up and follow Him to who knows where.

Really? No introduction?

Jesus could have been like, "Hey dude ... I'm the Messiah? Tax collecting is lame. Everyone hates you. Follow me and be loved (and likely martyred decades from now)."

No, Jesus just leans down, looks him in the eyes and says the most direct and life altering statement imaginable. And what did

Matthew do? Did he hesitate ... grip a bit tighter on his money bags? Nope. He hopped to his feet and left his wealth and position behind him forever.

Unbelievable.

One of the most intriguing things about Jesus' tax-collector outreach was His total disregard for outward appearance or social perception. These Old Testament IRS agents were swindling crooks with hardly a speck of decency. On the spectrum from "likely to love God," to "total pagan destined for hell," tax collectors surely fell far towards the latter end. And everyone knew it. Why did Jesus insist on reaching out to such losers?

Seems He proved them wrong every time.

But in all honesty, we do the same thing, looking at the outward appearance of folks and predicting their response to the gospel. For some reason we conclude that if someone is wild, then surely they would have no interest in Jesus. So we end up tight-lipped and silent and fail to even share a word about God's abundance, just because we assume them resistant, if not hostile, to the message. But throughout the life of Jesus we see Him reaching out to the most unlikely types of people.

Think about your own life, how Jesus reached into your world, offering grace and mercy and love and acceptance. It wasn't because you finally learned how to pray correctly. Or read your Bible enough. It was because Jesus interrupted your dead-end journey. He opened your eyes to His goodness, and you couldn't resist.

Everyone has their own story. Their own unexpected moment of rescue. In the next chapter, we'll look at how Jesus once again reached into a broken life and changed an entire city.

4

FOLLOW
ME

Imagine the picture: In the middle of a blazing hot day, Jesus walks up to a well, weary from a long journey, and sits down to rest. Soon a local woman approaches on the path, carrying a water jug on her shoulder. It is an unusual time of day for such a chore, the sweltering heat almost too much to bear. But she nears the well undeterred, ignoring the man who sits nearby and eyes her curiously.

As the rope lowers into darkness toward cool waters underground, she keeps her face down and wonders why the man is there. She knows what He must be thinking of her—He a Jew and she a Samaritan. She is hardly worthy to be spoken to. And if He knew of her life, He might just stone her himself. Plenty of others had threatened as much. For years she'd come to the well in the heat of day to avoid the eyes and the tongues of those who thought her wicked.

But here was this man.

She pulled water up from the depths, hand over hand, and suddenly He spoke.

"Will you give me a drink?"

Shocked, she froze, hardly lifting her eyes to Him. "You are a Jew and I am a Samaritan woman. How can you ask me for a drink?"

The man stared at her in silence for a moment, His eyes so clear and unmoving it was as if He peered right into the depths of her soul. "If you knew the gift of God and who it is that asks you for a drink, you would have asked Him and He would have given you living water."

"Sir," she said, seeing His empty hands, "you have nothing to draw with and the well is deep. Where can you get this living water? Are you greater than our father Jacob, who gave us the well and drank from it himself, as did also his sons and his livestock?"

"Everyone who drinks this water will be thirsty again," He said, motioning to the well, "but whoever drinks the water I give them will never thirst. Indeed, the water I give them will become in them a spring of water welling up to eternal life."

The words reached her ears, but she hardly understood them. All she could think of was the slight chance of avoiding these cumbersome trips to the well. If the man's words about this living water were true, she would never have to endure the heat again.

"Sir, give me this water so that I won't get thirsty and have to keep coming here to draw water."

The man paused, then spoke words that cut her to the quick. "Go, call your husband and come back."

She looked down upon the sandy gravel at her feet. "I have no husband."

"You are right when you say you have no husband. The fact is, you have had five husbands, and the man you now have is not your husband. What you have said is quite true."

The man's words seemed to linger in the air after He spoke. Each of them were spoken not with harsh judgment, but with a kind of gentle understanding that she had never heard before. She slowly lifted her gaze from the ground and looked upon him.

He was smiling.

"Sir," the woman said. "I can see that you are a prophet. Our ancestors worshipped on this mountain, but you Jews claim that the place where we must worship is in Jerusalem."

"Woman," Jesus replied, "believe Me, a time is coming when you will worship the Father neither on this mountain nor in Jerusalem. You Samaritans worship what you do not know; we worship what we do know, for salvation is from the Jews. Yet a time is coming and has now come when the true worshippers will worship the Father in the Spirit and in truth, for they are the kind of worshipers the Father seeks. God is spirit, and His worshipers must worship in the Spirit and in truth."

"I know the Messiah is coming," the woman said. "When He comes, He will explain everything to us."

A smile spread across the face of Jesus as He spoke the following words, "I, the one speaking to you, I am He."

The woman had just encountered the Savior. Her Savior. The very One who could rescue her from a lifetime of sin. She stares at Him, speechless, until she hears the sound of many others approaching, their sandals crunching on gravel. When they emerge from a bend in the path and see Jesus talking with the woman, their faces drop with shock.

What was He talking to such a woman for?

Before they ask a single question, she leaves her water jug behind and rushes past them toward the city. She has to tell as many as she can about who she has just met. A man who knew everything about her. A man who did not judge, did not condemn, but offered a gift of eternal life.

Could this possibly be the Messiah?

She runs into the town and tells everyone what she had seen, and as a result, the entire community comes out to see Jesus.

She might be one of the most effective instant evangelists in all of scripture.

"Many of the Samaritans from that town believed in him because of the woman's testimony, 'He told me everything I ever did.' So when the Samaritans came to him, they urged him to stay with them, and he stayed two days. And because of his words many more became believers. They said to the woman, 'We no longer believe just because of what you said; now we have heard for ourselves, and we know that this man really is the Savior of the world.'"

- John 4:39-42

People's openness to Jesus cannot be determined by their outward appearance or countenance. Some of the most radical and devoted followers are those who have been forgiven much. Some of the greatest evangelists are the ones who come from a sordid past. They are so thankful to be liberated that they share the good news as truly good news, not just as canned words on a tract.

Jesus constantly disregarded outward appearances during His ministry. He reached out to a demon-possessed man in a graveyard for crying out loud! Talk about creepy. But the guy was totally delivered from his bondage and wanted nothing more than to follow Jesus wherever He went.

And what about Saul? He was a man of violence and cruelty, but Jesus confronts him on the road, knocks him to the ground, and speaks directly to his heart. He changes his name and sets him on a totally new course. As a result, Saul (now Paul) becomes the greatest apostle, who wrote the majority of the New Testament letters.

What if Jesus had considered him too intense? Too unpredictable? Too angry? We'd have a massive chunk of the Bible left unwritten, and many churches left unplanted in the first century. All of Christian history would have changed. Jesus chose Paul even in his rage and hatred.

I think of some of the guys in our church who come from violent gangs. Their lives have been radically changed, and now God is using them to share the gospel all over the city. What if we had considered them too far away from God to be reached? Further lives would have been left untouched. You never know who God is going to save and use.

Thinking back to Matthew in the previous chapter, when Matthew agrees to follow Jesus, Jesus doesn't recommend joining a seminary or starting a prayer group. He tells him to throw a party. And that very day as Jesus is hanging out at His new friend's house, the Bible tells us, *"Many tax collectors and sinners came and were reclining with Jesus and his disciples." (Matthew 9:10)*

All of a sudden Matthew's crazy group of friends start crowding in just to be near Jesus. I find it hard to believe that these same folks would have hiked up to hear Jesus' sermon on the mount. But they *would* go to a party ... and one with a famous prophet as the guest of honor was all the better. The Bible tells us clearly that 'sinners gathered around Jesus.'

Now let me ask you a question. How many Christians do you know that just have sinners gathering around them? Probably not many. We spend so much energy sheltering ourselves from the world, it's like we walk around in a bubble. But if we tapped into God's heart for people, our eyes opening to those around us, I believe we'd become magnetic. People would simply want to be with us because they'd sense something different about us. Why are we joyful? Why do we love people so well? Our countenance points them to Jesus.

Another thing to note is that Jesus was there with His disciples. He rarely did things alone. I'm sure the Son of God didn't need these guys all that much, but He chose to have them along wherever He went. Perhaps He hoped to model the value of working as a team. If we want to impact the world, we must do so with a family of like-minded people. Don't try to go it alone. I assure you it makes the whole endeavor a great deal easier.

We've got to have a *Party Posse*.

Who are the folks in your life who could join you to reach out to your community? Who could share the same Kingdom vision? Lock arms with them and start changing the world!

During college I was part of a national fraternity. As God continued to work in my heart, I grew uneasy about the common practice of rush. Most of you know the drill. We reach out to a bunch of eager freshman and sophomores, build them up and woo them in, and then at the end of a few weeks, we gather together and vote on the ones deemed cool enough to become members.

Not like Jesus.

I contemplated quitting the club altogether. Then Jesus gave me an idea: at these parties tons of young men come. They long to fit in and belong. The fraternity will evaluate them by outward appearance and first impressions. But I could actually seek out the hurting and needy and insecure and spend time with them. I could encourage them and speak destiny over their lives and make them feel loved and treasured.

I could tell them about Jesus.

Instantly I set out on a secret, undercover Kingdom mission inside my fraternity. I got together a few of my friends with similar vision and shared my plan.

"Guys, tonight at the party, let's pray and reach out to the guys that no one else wants to talk to."

That night, as the fraternity band pounded out their songs, the air thick with tobacco smoke, my friends and I started telling guys how much they were loved and that God had a destiny for their lives. They had not come expecting to hear about Jesus at all, but they went home struck anew with the goodness of God.

For us, this was a party with purpose.

And I promise there are more to be had.

Think about it. Hardly anyone is thinking about Jesus at a typical party. Almost everyone is insecure and eager to strike up conversation so they're not the loner "reject" in the corner. Talk with them. Listen to their story. Share your own. Let the joy of God radiate from you like a neon lamp! Some people might think you're from another planet, but I bet you nine times out of ten, those folks will go home with something stirring in their souls. They might forget the music and the dancing, but they won't forget the way you loved them, listened to them, and pointed them to the Savior.

Why does Jesus go to parties?

"When the Pharisees saw this, they asked his disciples, 'Why does your teacher eat with tax collectors and sinners?' On hearing this, Jesus said, 'It is not the healthy who need a doctor, but the sick. But go and learn what this means: 'I desire mercy, not sacrifice.' For I have not come to call the righteous, but sinners.'"
- Matthew 9:12-13

He went to parties because that's where the sinners were. He knew what His mission was, to reach the sick, lost, and dying. What good was it for Him to hang out with spiritual leaders all the time? They thought they knew everything. They didn't really even like Him. Some hated Him so much they wanted Him dead.

Jesus knew exactly whom He wanted to reach out to. The lowest of the low. The broken and weary. Those with nowhere else to turn.

So get your *Party Posse,* put your heads together and find out which parties you're supposed to 'crash' with the love of God.

So often we divide our lives into two groups—sacred and secular—and Jesus is only welcome in one. But I'm here to say that Jesus isn't just meant to be talked about in church. He can infuse every area of your life. Jesus wants to go with us everywhere. He wants to use us far more than we assume. Don't neglect these opportunities. They often prove infinitely more effective than the most dynamic church service in the world.

Jesus loves to be invited into things: our work, our school, our challenging relationships. Jesus longs to be present, to be invited. No area should be off limits.

In the gospels we always see Jesus showing up where people asked him to come. Think about the wedding in John chapter two.

"On the third day a wedding took place at Cana in Galilee. Jesus' mother was there, and Jesus and his disciples had also been invited to the wedding."
- John 2:1-2

And now for one of the craziest and dare I say unorthodox moments in Jesus' ministry.

"When the wine was gone, Jesus' mother said to him, 'They have no more wine.' 'Woman, why do you involve me?' Jesus replied. 'My hour has not yet come.'"
- John 2:3-4

I would pay huge money to have a hidden camera at this event. Here is Jesus with His mom, the wine runs out, and

Mommy delivers the news with a little wink-wink. What was Jesus' expression at this point?

She didn't come out and bark an order. Just kind of threw a bit of suggestive bait as moms are prone to do. Did Jesus roll his eyes? Probably not. Did He glance back at His disciples and shrug His shoulders? Perhaps. Regardless, He went from 'What's it to me?' to doing something about it within a few seconds.

Let's ponder this a moment. Jesus, the Son of God, had no apparent intention to do anything about the wine problem. But, because His Mom hinted that He should ... because she invited Him to make something happen, He did, as we'll see in the next verse. Why? Because He loved His mother. He cared about her request. Just like He cares about ours. The Bible says in the book of James, *"You have not because you ask not."* God wants to bless us because He loves us. And often we miss out on deeper blessing because we fail to ask God for much at all. He likes to be asked. He likes specificity, not a gray, generic prayer He can't sink his divinity into. Give Him something to answer; then stand back and watch!

Jesus can't resist blessing people when they ask and believe.

So Mary asks Him to play bartender, and what happens next is borderline scandalous to some modern day religious thinking.

"His mother said to the servants, 'Do whatever he tells you.' Nearby stood six stone water jars, the kind used by the Jews for ceremonial washing, each holding from twenty to thirty gallons. Jesus said to the servants, 'Fill the jars with water'; so they filled them to the brim. Then he told them, 'Now draw some out and take it to the master of the banquet.' They did so, and the master of the banquet tasted the water that had been turned into wine. He did not realize where it had come from, though the servants who had drawn the water knew. Then he called the bridegroom aside

and said, 'Everyone brings out the choice wine first and then the
cheaper wine after the guests have had too much to drink; but you
have saved the best till now.'"
  - John 2:5-10

I don't think it's a coincidence that the first place He chooses to do a miracle is at a party. He's a genius. If I was Him, I would have calculated the perfect timing for the booze to run out so things wouldn't get wild. Aunt Matilda wouldn't get up on the table and do her crazy Jewish dance like she always does when she has too much wine. No one's going to crash a camel on the way home. We'd have just enough to enjoy ourselves and not an ounce more. All would be good and perfect and predictable.

But that's not what the Son of God does.

Jesus says, *This isn't good that the wine's out. I'm going to make more and it's going to be so much better.*

Now hear me very carefully. I am NOT trying to make a big case for alcohol. The Bible is very clear about not getting drunk with wine, which leads to debauchery; we're called to be filled with the Holy Spirit instead.

The point I'm making is simple. Some of us have this idea that Jesus sits sternly in heaven with a naughty and nice list and spends the vast majority of time just scrutinizing your every activity. We imagine that the moment you make a mistake, He leans over with a scowl and scratches a jagged x-mark on the naughty list and shakes His head in disappointment. We think Jesus is freaked out that we're going to do something bad and misrepresent Him.

But then I think about what kind of dad I strive to be.

As a father, I don't say, "Put my kids in a padded room and get them away from anything dangerous or questionable because then, they'll be safe! Nothing will happen to them!" That's not how I am. I actually let them take risks. I let them jump off a cliff into a lake. I let my eight-year-old boy (GASP!) shoot a BB gun. Why? Because I want my kids to know adventure. I want them to have the abundant life. I want them to say that being a Herber was fun.

And here's Jesus saying, *You know what? I want you to see that I want to bless you, people at this party. And I want you to know that My blessing is actually way better than anything in this world. I can take anything in the world and I give it an upgrade. Because I'm the author of the party.*

So what happens next?

"What Jesus did here in Cana of Galilee was the first of the signs through which he revealed his glory; and his disciples believed in him."
- John 2:11

Why did Jesus love parties?

Because Jesus loves to bless! For when He does such things, it brings Him glory. It raises weary eyes to heaven and lightens hearts. It brings hope to hopeless situations. It points people to God.

Let me tell you a little story of how I've experienced this in my own life.

After college I went through a discipleship training school at my church, to be equipped to better walk with God and reach out to others. I was going through it with my best friend Robert Fuller. Now, at the time, Robert was struggling with discouragement now and then, working at a local restaurant and trying his best to provide for himself.

One evening on the way to work he noticed a car in front of

him had his initials, RLF, on its license plate. Almost on a whim, he asked God that every time he saw his initial on a license plate, it would be God telling him He was loved. The car drove on, he went to work and didn't think much more of it. Then the next day, he saw it again on another car and instantly remembered his prayer. He was encouraged, to say the least.

But things were just getting started.

The next day he saw it again. And the next day, again. Again and again and again. One day, weeks later, he saw his initials *six times* in a row, three of which were seen within a ten second span. He told me he almost punched a hole in the roof of his car he was so pumped up. And no lie, people, for two years he saw it almost everyday. It sounds too good to be true. A freak coincidence. All I know is he asked for something ... a kind of blessing ... and Jesus more than answered his prayer.

I was so struck by this little miracle I asked the same thing for myself. And you know how many times I saw my initials on a license plate the first day? Zip! Second day, zilch! Third day, zero! I have NEVER seen my initials on a license plate. So one day I prayed, "God, I'm pretty sure you love, me too. Can You just show me Your love in a unique way?" I asked God what sign I should ask for and I got a mental impression of a red balloon. Okay, I thought, who doesn't like balloons? But I didn't tell a soul about what I'd prayed. I went to the training school that day and opened up the door to the offices and the whole floor was covered in about a hundred red balloons. My knees buckled, my eyes filled with tears. A staff member saw me freaking out and asked me if I was okay.

"Red balloons ..." I stammered, looking quite the awkward fool.

But God was showing me His love, just like I'd asked. Not long after that I was leading my first mission trip and dealing with some pretty acute insecurity.

"God," I prayed. "I need to know You're with me because I feel totally ill-equipped. I can't do this."

I walked into a Wendy's on the way to the airport with my team, heart pounding with this new and daunting responsibility, and I stopped in the line and gave out a big sigh. Throwing my head back in the process, I noticed, right above me ... smack dab over my head ... wait for it ... a red balloon.

I was filled with almost instant courage.

I cannot tell you how many times I've seen red balloons over the years. I've walked out of business meetings and seen a random red balloon bouncing along the road right in front of me. I've opened up closet doors only to find a red balloon staring me in the face. The other day I was hiking in the woods, and right in the middle of the trail (you guessed it) was a red balloon.

Hard to believe, but it's all true.

Jesus was telling me 'I love you' over and over and over again in my own personalized-especially-for-Robert kind of way. I've shared this story through the years and many people have been challenged to ask for the same thing—their own specific 'sign'. People have come up to me weeping, sharing their story of how God showed them His love in the same way.

This is why He showed up to parties. This is why He performed miracles. He wants us to know He is madly in love with people. He jumps into our world to pursue us and to say, 'Hey, I'm here and I want you to draw near to Me because in My presence is fullness of joy.' It's imperative that we understand this, because when we do, it doesn't just usher us into the abundant life—we also become people who radiate the same truth, drawing people by the truckload into God's Kingdom party.

5

YOUR ROLE IN THE PARTY

Okay. We're going to do a little experiment. It's a simple test. When I say a word, you tell me the first feeling it triggers. Ready? Here we go.

Mexican food.

I'm pretty confident the mere thought of chips and queso, tamales, and luscious enchiladas only elicit feelings of mouthwatering delight. That's exactly how it should be. Well done.

Now, for another word.

Disney.

I'm sure right now everyone is filled with childlike nostalgia as they think about cartoons and theme parks and wishing upon a star. I mean who doesn't like a good Disney flick or a vacation to the most magical place on earth? I'm guilty of both.

Time for the last word.

Evangelism.

Ooooohhhh! I left-hooked ya! For some, this word reminds you of awkward door to door exchanges, of flipping nervously through a tract. Others may only recall the terrified nausea of trying to share the gospel with a stranger.

Few of us, I'm liable to bet, get all pumped and excited about the whole concept. We know it's right. We're commanded to shine the light and make disciples. But the idea can so often feel like forced salesmanship.

I understand. I've been there.

But let's break it down to its simplest, least intimidating form.

Evangelism is simply telling others about your relationship with Jesus.

You don't have to be a charismatic preacher or eloquent speaker. You don't even have to be a people person. You just have to be a human being with a pulse and a belief in Jesus Christ. Are you able to make conversation? Just relax and smile and act like you've got something awesome to share, which you do! And not only that, your words, no matter how stammered or awkward, have the power to change someone's life forever. Remember, God uses the foolish things to shame the wise. He's the one at work anyway. The pressure is off.

In my early days of walking with God I made some pretty big blunders in the area of evangelism. A gospel sharing pro I was not. I'd go to church and hear about how awesome God was, how awesome heaven was going to be forever and ever and ever for those who believed in Jesus. And then I'd hear about hell. How those who don't know Jesus are destined for a Christ-less eternity, for weeping and gnashing of teeth where the fires are never quenched.

Not pretty.

So in my youthful zeal, armed with such truth, I thought about different friends of mine who didn't know Jesus. Naturally, I did not want them going to the bad place forever and ever. I had to warn them, as any good friend should.

I'll never forget the first time I tried to "evangelize."

It was at my friend John's house. We'd had a great day hanging out and doing a whole lot of nothing when the thought struck me that John didn't know Jesus. With this somber realization I turned to him and said, "Hey man ... we've had a great day today ... but I've got to tell you something. You're going to hell."

He looked back at me, more than a little confused.

"You're going to hell and I'm going to heaven. You're going to die in your sin so you need to accept Jesus right now to keep that from happening."

Could I have been more direct in my good news delivery? I think not. Alas, my friend wasn't happy. And I'm sorry to say after I left his house that day our friendship never recovered. For some reason he didn't take my mention of his eternal damnation well. Go figure.

What was the problem? Why didn't he fall on his knees with tears streaming down his face and accept Jesus right then and there as I pulled out a guitar and led us in a hymn? Well, for one, John likely looked at my life and saw no difference whatsoever between the two of us. Ironically, he was actually a better guy than me at the time. More moral. More respectful towards adults. When I told him that hell was his one-way destination, he probably thought I was the biggest hypocrite ever.

I'm sure many of you have experienced similar crashes and burns when it comes to sharing your faith. Your heart's not bad—it's actually well motivated—but maybe you've burned some people along the way in your zealous attempt to bring them into the fold. And I'd venture to say that in response to your past failures, some of you have pretty much given up. You think maybe you're not cut out for this evangelism stuff, leaving it to the Billy Grahams of the world with their clear and effective strategies and gifting. You decide to just live a good life in the hopes that someone at some point will just spontaneously come to Christ through observing how nice you are.

But what often happens is that many people in our spheres never get to hear about Jesus because of our silence. People in our workplace, in our families, on our kids' sports teams. Think of how many of them need to know Jesus, but have no way of really hearing about Him ... besides through you. Still, we fail to speak of the joy within us, or the glorious hope of Jesus Christ.

Thankfully, there is grace. Even through our awkward bumblings, people can be touched. I think about one relationship where I had a measure of success in sharing Jesus, though I actually kind of stumbled into the effort. It was with my friend Teddy. He was my best friend growing up and, like John, was a great guy.

Then one time we were having an event at our church called Disciple Now, where kids in the youth group would gather together for a huge rally with a rocked out worship band and a young, dynamic guest speaker who really connected with kids about the gospel. There were games and lots of teenage craziness. Each night we'd split off into smaller groups and go to different people's homes for a kind of sleepover with lots of food, more fun, and hours and hours of hangout time. College students would come in and help lead the kids at each home, which to us junior high schoolers was equivalent to a celebrity visit.

Thinking he'd enjoy the time, I invited Teddy. And over the course of the weekend he had an absolute blast. Not just with the games and music and food, but when the leaders would share about Jesus and talk about their lives, Teddy was totally engaged with them, listening intently. At the end of the weekend I was blown away as Teddy gave his life to Jesus. To this day, twenty-five years later, Teddy is still walking with God.

Successful evangelism? Check.

I've often thought about these two guys, comparing the different methods of sharing Jesus with them. One was an obvious fail, while the other a resounding and time-tested success. What was the difference?

When I look back at Luke 14 I get some insight. Jesus was at a (you guessed it) dinner party and a man was talking to Him about a feast in the Kingdom of God. Jesus responded by telling a story about another feast. Now remember that Jesus' parables were almost always about Father God and His Kingdom.

"A certain man was preparing a great banquet and invited many guests. At the time of the banquet he sent his servant to tell those who had been invited, 'Come, for everything is now ready.' But they all alike began to make excuses. The first said, 'I have just bought a field, and I must go and see it. Please excuse me.' Another said, 'I have just bought five yoke of oxen, and I'm on my way to try them out. Please excuse me.' Still another said, 'I just got married, so I can't come.' The servant came back and reported this to his master. Then the owner of the house became angry and ordered his servant, 'Go out quickly into the streets and alleys of the town and bring in the poor, the crippled, the blind and the lame.' 'Sir,' the servant said, 'what you ordered has been done, but there is still room.' Then the master told his servant, 'Go out to the roads and country lanes and compel them to come in, so that my house will be full. I tell you, not one of those who were invited will get a taste of my banquet.'"
- *Luke 14:16-24*

This is called the parable of the great banquet. And I believe there are many beautiful aspects of Father God that Jesus unpacks for us here. Let's go through them one by one.

God is a party thrower.

When you think about God, does this idea cross your mind? Most of us would probably answer 'no.' The vast majority of humans think God is more like a white wigged judge with a giant gavel and a black robe, ready to pound us into the ground for being such idiots with our lives. We see a scowler. Not a partier. Not a celebrator. Not a warm, fun-loving host. But, according to scripture, He is a partying God. Why? Because He loves to bless people. He loves to draw people into His home.

The Father has an abundance.

This parable doesn't just say it was a dinner party ... it was a GREAT banquet. I was looking at the word 'great' in the text, and in going back to the original Greek the translated word is actually megas ... where we get the word MEGA! It was a mega party. Not just crackers and cheese and punch. We're talking about a big time buffet with a pasta bar and big slab of roast beef, sushi, and a whole table devoted to desserts. Our God is a mega God who throws mega feasts for breakfast.

Do you see God as a God of abundance? When you see someone else get blessed do you get that painful jolt to the side as you think to yourself, *Oh no ... they got blessed.* Which means I have less a chance to get blessed as well. We're all human, so we've all been guilty of envy in the face of another's blessing. But pain caused by someone else's blessing is a sure sign that we doubt God's abundance. We assume that He has a limited amount of goodness to divvy out.

It makes me think of those humanitarian relief helicopters swooping down to some famine stricken country. The chopper descends over a roiling crowd of starving refugees, tossing out bags of rice and bottled water, totally incapable of meeting everyone's needs. And the people flail about, elbows to faces, clawing for just a handful of rice and a mouthful of water. Most leave disappointed.

This is NOT how God operates. He pulls in a fleet of food trucks to the hungry horde and tosses out hoagies and tacos and burgers and falafel until everyone is so full they can hardly do anything but curl up for a nap. When someone else gets blessed, rejoice, because their blessing comes from the same God as yours. It should actually make you happier. If God can do that for them, then why not for me?

God is abundant. Do you have an abundance mentality? Or one of lack? Of more than enough? Or of scarcity? When someone gets a word from God, or gets prayed for ... do you internally fret because you automatically assume that your chances for the same have been decreased? False! When someone else gets financially blessed, do you grumble that others always get blessed and you don't? Open your eyes! If God blesses someone else, He can bless you too. This is how God wants us to view Him.

Abundant.

More than enough.

God sends out many invitations.

Many invitations. I'm no English major, but I'm pretty sure the word 'many' means a lot. Now, if you want to get me mad as a pastor, talk about how God has just invited a *few* people into His Kingdom. That's actually a big discussion going on in the body of Christ these days. But the Bible speaks otherwise. In this parable, Jesus is painting a picture of Father God. And it says many guests were invited.

Still don't believe me?

Let's visit one of the best known verses in the entire Bible.

In John 3:16 does it say, *For God so loved the few, that He gave His only Son?'* No! God so loved The World. Everyone. All of us. So He sent Jesus as a living invitation into His Kingdom.

What about this verse: *This is good and pleases God our savior. Who wants a few people to be saved.*

Once again ... NO! That's not what it says. It says God wants ALL PEOPLE to be saved. I don't care what kind of theological bent you have, whether you know Greek or Hebrew or Swahili. You can't get around this direct communication.

Everyone.

All people.

Many.

Seems pretty inclusive if you ask me. God's hasn't created some secret club with private invitations. It's the grandest party the world has ever known.

Now let me be clear. Am I saying that all people will be saved? Sadly, no. Only those who believe in and receive Jesus into their hearts will be saved for eternity. But the gift of salvation is offered to everyone by Father God. This is undeniable.

Every person you see walking down the street was made by God. And God longs to draw them to Himself. Every person in your workplace. Every person in your family. All have an invitation. Will they all choose God? Will they all respond to the invitation? No. But the invitation stands, nonetheless.

The Father is pro-active in gathering people.

He doesn't just fling out invitations and hope the postal service does its job. God takes an active role in the process. He sends out His servants. And as we look at this parable, who do the servants represent?

Us! All believers.

As a follower of Jesus, I've been given the grand privilege of telling people about the Gospel ... of handing out party invitations. If this part of my life is truly as wonderful and life giving as I claim, how could I not share it with others? That would be like winning the lottery, then being given a stack of additional winning tickets with the simple command to pass them out to everyone I see. Would I keep them for myself? Would I sit at home and simply count my winnings? No way! I'd be passing out tickets as fast as I could.

This is what changed my entire view on evangelism. Growing up in the Bible Belt I used to think the world was always having its crazy party of constant fun, and there I was, like a spy for Jesus, sneaking up on different folks until I could get close enough to bop them on the head with my Bible and command them to cut it out! Quit having so much fun. Come to my church and sit in a pew. I truly thought this was my duty: to show people the error of their debauchery and lead them into the fluffy fold of God where we could tell each other how awful the world is.

We are the servants, tasked with inviting everyone to God's party.

A party that so far exceeds anything the world has to offer, it's almost comical (if it wasn't so tragic). God's party is the true party, with real food, real music, real fun. The world's party, by comparison, is nothing more than a mud puddle with stale bread and a guy playing a broken kazoo in the corner. Most have never known anything different, so they party harder and harder just to make themselves feel happy for a fleeting moment.

Jesus is their way of escape, their rescue.

And we hold His message like a torch in a cave.

If we understood the world this way, would we remain silent? Would we keep Jesus' invitation tucked away just so we don't sound preachy or awkward? I believe if we comprehended the beauty of God's party and the power of the invitation, we'd hardly let a day go by without passing them on.

And it's not just about heaven, folks. So much of our evangelism centers on where we'll go when we die. But the Bible says that the Kingdom is now. The party doesn't start when we croak. The music's already playing. The food is already hot. When we invite people into God's party we're talking present tense. He is ready and willing to change lives here and now. That's what He offers. Eternity begins today.

As we invite people, we do it with joy, with a smile on our faces because we know what it is we offer.

David says in Psalm 23 that God *'Has brought me to His banqueting table.'*

Not, *will bring*, but *brought*. As in, already happened. Done deal.

So as we go out and share, we invite people into a present day party.

But something very interesting happens when people are invited. Looking at the parable, we see one primary reason for declining the invitation, and it's not what you would expect. It doesn't say people grew angry and beat down the servants with clubs. They were actually polite in their responses.

What kept them away, then?

Distractions.

Someone bought an ox. Someone bought a field. Someone just got married. So they don't have time to party. Now, there's nothing wrong with fields. Or oxen. And thankfully there's nothing wrong with getting married because I love my wife.

So what's the problem?

One application could be about possessions. Again, possessions in and of themselves are not wrong. But as we all know, sometimes possessions can possess us, rather than the other way around. The guy who bought the field was not in sin because he wanted some land. He was just so in love with his new plot of dirt that he blew off a chance to enjoy a grand banquet with an all-you-can-eat buffet and a mariachi band. He'd rather walk around on his land.

Is there any possession that has taken hold of you? Something you think about more than anything else, even God? If so, you might need a little soul check.

What do the oxen represent? Work. This is a big one for Americans. As a general rule, we're cultural go-getters. Our ancestors carved a life out of the new world, for crying out loud. Working our tails off and striving for more is simply in our blood. But work can easily become an obsession if we're not careful. It can become a kind of god, distracting us from God's best in our lives. The guy in the parable could only use one yoke of oxen at a time, not five. But he insisted he had to try them out at once. It's likely the party was at night too, so either homeboy decided to try his new animals out by torchlight or he just wanted to stare at them in the barn as they munched on hay. Who knows?

If you asked your family right now what they thought mattered most to you, would your work be first on the list? Even over God and His Kingdom? I assure you, no amount of money or power will ever come close to filling your heart like God can.

Finally, what about the newlywed? Was this relationship the most important thing in his life? Many of us consider our marriages to be the top priority in our lives. And though it is huge ... it's not number one. I'd venture to say that marriages where the relationship is of chief importance are not as strong as you might think. If God is not paramount, the relationship will weaken bit by bit, like a dam with cracks creeping through the concrete.

Your marriage should make you more effective in the

Kingdom. Your friendships should make you stronger in God, rather than drawing you away. Relationships are a gift from God. But don't place the gift on the throne of your life, for the enemy will seize every chance he can get to pull you away from the King and His abundant life.

As we read on in the parable, the plot thickens.

The servants go back to give a report of what happened and the owner of the house, the party host, gets angry. Yes. Angry. I know we've been talking about the partying God and how much He loves us and wants to bless us like crazy, and you probably think my total view of God is like a good-natured grandpa who spends all of His time passing out candy and giving horsey rides on his knee. But the fact is, God gets angry. Sobering, yes. But true.

He got angry.

Why?

Were his feelings hurt? Maybe His pride? So He throws a little God-tantrum when He hears about all these meanies ditching His invitation? Nope. I believe the parable teaches us that God gets angry when we reject His invitation because we miss out on His best. As a father I would be furious if I spent all day preparing a huge party and building an incredible tree house in my backyard and my kids refused to come because they were playing with dead roaches in the sewer. I wouldn't want them to miss out! God is a billion times more passionate about this very thing. He knows the beauty of what He offers—what He has prepared. He knows that nothing in all of reality can possibly compare. So when we, in our colossal ignorance, choose other things, it seems utterly foolish.

A pretty cool thing here in the story is that, even in his anger, the master doesn't respond like most of us would. He doesn't tell his servants to go back to the same people and tell them how stupid they are. He doesn't lash out. His anger is actually channeled into something greater. He becomes even more proactive and tells His servants to go out into the streets and invite the poor, the cripple, the blind, and the lame. When people reject God, He casts the net even wider.

This has really been our heart at All Peoples Church. I remember when I first moved to San Diego and different pastors would warn me that this city is a very hard place to plant a church. People have the beach. They have their hobbies. They live in a veritable paradise. What need do they have for Jesus, much less church? But we, as a staff, made a decision to focus on the poor and the broken and the ones who were in need. Within the first eight months of our church, we saw one hundred twenty people make decisions to give their lives to Jesus.

Why such fruit?

Is it because we're such great strategist and super skilled evangelist?

Nope.

I truly believe it's because God has called us to the hurting and the broken and the needy and He's always faithful to His word.

We take Isaiah 61:1 to heart.

"The Spirit of the Sovereign Lord is on me, because the Lord has anointed me to proclaim good news to the poor. He has sent me to bind up the brokenhearted, to proclaim freedom for the captives and release from from darkness for the prisoners."
- Isaiah 61:1

I want to challenge all of us to have this kind of mindset in every area of our lives. Open your eyes in your workplaces. In your family. Among your friends. You'll find plenty of people who aren't interested in God because of their distractions. But you'll also find the hurting and the broken. Reach out to these people. Listen to their stories. Share with them how Jesus has changed your life and can change their lives as well.

Invite them to the party.

If the church would keep its eyes and ears and hearts open to the hurting and the broken, the world would change faster than we could imagine. Campuses would be transformed. Workplaces would be flooded with life. Broken families would be healed. As people come into the loving, joy-filled banquet of God, reality itself is changed from darkness to light.

But we must remember our place in the party.

One of the blessings I had growing up was that my grandparents were very wealthy. They had a beautiful property with a mansion and a pool and a nice pond to fish in—lots of fun things for a young boy to do. Years later, when I started following God, I wanted others to be blessed by the place. Because I knew my grandparents were generous, and they loved to serve people, when missionary families would come back from overseas and needed a vacation, I would invite them to spend a few days in the guest house. There, they could take long walks in nature, go fishing, swim in the pool, and just enjoy themselves without spending a dime. It was so much fun seeing family after family take us up on the offer and later tell us it was the best vacation they'd ever had.

It had nothing to do with me. It wasn't my generosity that got them there. I just delivered the invitation. That's how we are in the Kingdom. We have a Father who is rich beyond imagination, with a heart so loving it can't be swayed, and we go out with confidence, knowing He is good, knowing He is gracious.

I want to take you into one last scripture. And it's a good one.

"On the last and greatest day of the festival, Jesus stood and said in a loud voice, 'Let anyone who is thirsty come to me and drink. Whoever believes in me, as Scripture has said, rivers of living water will flow from within them.'"

- John 7:37-38

Jesus shows up, yet again, at another party. And on the last day, after everyone has stuffed their faces for days and consumed gallons of whatever festive beverage was on tap, He comes out and shouts for all to hear: *Hey everybody! If you're still hungry ... if you're still thirsty ... it's because the world's food will never satisfy you. So come to me and I'll fill you up like nothing ever has! I want to give you a drink that not only flows into you, but flows out of you.*

Living water. The Holy Spirit.

We'll talk about this in the next chapter.

Get ready. The party's about to explode.

6

THE PARTY WITHIN

In the dusty border town of Juarez, Mexico something happened to me that changed my life forever.

It was my junior year of college, spring break, and the first foreign mission trip I'd ever taken part in. For months I'd been hearing about this trip taken by a local church, how every year hundreds of people were saved. I was even more intrigued by the report of dozens being miraculously healed. I signed up out of simple curiosity. I'd been on mission trips before: a choir tour one year when the only evident fruit was a third grader who recommitted his life to Jesus after a puppet show. And then there was the trip to Arizona where we spent a week reroofing a church. I don't think I shared once about Jesus, much less prayed for anyone. But the place sure was pretty.

Riding the bus west across the Texan desert toward Mexico, I was eager to see God move with my own eyes. If the stories were true, Mexico must be the Disney's Magical World of mission trips. I half expected to venture into the streets and see people come to Jesus the moment I opened my mouth. And as far as healings ... I was ready to have my mind blown.

The first day of the trip we hit the ground running, pockets loaded with gospel tracts, expectant and full of faith. I remember walking into a city park, scanning the crowds and trying to pick the softest looking people—those sure to accept Jesus with gusto. If people looked mean or shady, I stepped past them as quickly as I could. Evangelism was scary enough; why pick someone who looked like they were about to mug me? Within minutes I spotted a guy who seemed pleasant enough. I walked up to him with the widest smile my cheek muscles could manage and said hello. He greeted me with a welcoming nod (good sign), so I pulled out a tract and took him through it page by page. Through every scripture and every main point, he nodded his understanding. Then, when the moment of glory arrived and I asked him if he wanted to accept Jesus, he looked at me flatly and responded with a simple "no."

Bummer.

Maybe he was harder than he looked. Oh well, I thought, on to the next person.

Once I found a second easy target, I pulled out another tract and repeated my smiling gospel presentation. And again, to my increasing dismay, the person responded with another big, fat "no"!

What was going on? Was I so bad at sharing the gospel that I couldn't lead people to the Lord in the most fertile soil imaginable? What a disgrace!

Thankfully, toward the end of the night, the leaders gathered us to pray for the sick. Okay, I thought, this is it. Now I can see God move in power. But as I started praying for different people ... nothing happened. Eventually I tried to change my methods, increasing the volume of my "In the name of Jesus" and "Amen," shifting the angle of my laid-on hands. Still, I felt about as effective as a praying mannequin. People kept right on being sick.

What was wrong with me?

Maybe you've felt this way too, some time or another—discouraged that you're not seeing God move the way you've read about in the Bible, or the way you've heard in other believers' experiences. You might feel a bit like a spiritual pip-squeak. A poser. A wannabe apostle or something.

That's exactly how I felt.

But what does Jesus have to say about this sort of thing?

In the book of Acts we see Jesus eating with His disciples and explaining what lies ahead for them. Now keep in mind, this is after He's been crucified and has risen from the grave. His followers are chilling out at a table with Him, enjoying a meal. That's when Jesus starts giving some instructions:

"On one occasion, while he was eating with them, he gave them this command: 'Do not leave Jerusalem, but wait for the gift my Father promised, which you have heard me speak about. For John baptized with water, but in a few days you will be baptized with the Holy Spirit.'"

- Acts 1:4-5

This is super interesting to me. I mean, if anyone was equipped to do the work of God, it was the disciples. They lived with Jesus for three years, for crying out loud. They walked with Him day in and day out. They heard hundreds of His sermons. They had seen Him heal the sick, cleanse the leaper, and cast out demons. They'd even been sent out on a short-term mission trip, on their own, with Jesus' blessing. These were the MVP's of Christendom. The first class. But instead of telling them to go and change the world right then and there, what did He tell them to do?

Wait.

Why?

A lot of people, upon reading this passage, mistakenly assume that Jesus said wait because the Holy Spirit was finally coming to earth. But that's not the case. A few pages earlier in the Gospels, when Jesus appeared before the disciples after His resurrection, it says in John 20:

"On the evening of that first day of the week, when the disciples were together, with the doors locked for fear of the Jewish leaders, Jesus came and stood among them and said, 'Peace be with you!' After he said this, he showed them his hands and side. The disciples were overjoyed when they saw the Lord.

Again Jesus said, 'Peace be with you! As the Father has sent me, I am sending you.' And with that he breathed on them and said, 'Receive the Holy Spirit.'"
- John 20:19-22

Okay. So why is Jesus talking to His disciples a while later in the book of Acts—a bunch of guys who have already 'received the Holy Spirit'—and saying 'Wait ... there's a gift that's coming. John baptized with water ... I'm going to baptize you with the Holy Spirit.' I believe it's because they were sealed by the Holy Spirit for salvation on the first occasion, but were empowered by the Holy Spirit on the second. Different segments within the church at large get all bent out of shape regarding the phrase 'Baptized with the Holy Spirit.' These words often conjure all sorts of weird notions about the so called 'charismatic churches' with their snake handling and crazy rituals, or maybe those three-piece suit wearing, hair-all-done-up televangelists who always seem to be asking for money. But let's take a more level-headed approach. This has nothing to do with style of worship or mode of expression. It really just boils down to our 'source' of strength and power. The gift Jesus was speaking about was "receiving power" from the Holy Spirit. Jesus explains its purpose in one of the most invigorating pump up verses in the Bible.

"But you will receive power when the Holy Spirit comes on you; and you will be my witnesses in Jerusalem, and in all Judea and Samaria, and to the ends of the earth."
- *Acts 1:8*

Now if that's not cool, I don't know what is.

Power. From. God.

I'll take that!

In our culture we have an ongoing fascination with super heroes. If Hollywood continues on its current moviemaking trajectory, studies show that eventually, 95% of all cinematic releases will be super hero flicks. Well, maybe not. I confess my fabricated statistic. But we can all agree that there will always be a steady stream of comic book, super hero movies as long as humans walk the earth. There's just something so intriguing about a normal person being gifted with a super power. It seems intrinsic in our DNA to desire power to help the helpless, to change history. God knit this desire into our very makeup. We long to break out of our limited resources, to surpass our weaknesses and take part in something bigger. When we see a broken and dying world, many of us just wish we could shoot spider webs out of our wrists, or have x-ray vision and the ability to fly supersonic ... just so we could help people.

But, I hate to break it to you—we will never fly. Even if we donned a cape and purple spandex, we'd still plummet to the earth and land in a heap of broken bones.

Sorry. But here's the real kicker, the mind-blowing truth: God wants to endow you with power. When the Holy Spirit comes upon you, power is inevitable.

Let's go back to Mexico and my lame attempts at sharing the gospel and praying for the sick.

Each morning we would gather at a local church to worship and hear a message from our college pastor, Jimmy Seibert (now the leader of the Antioch International Movement of Churches). I remember sitting on the back row of the sanctuary, bummed out beyond belief, staring glumly over the heads of two hundred other college students who all seemed to be experiencing God in powerful ways. Feeling like a spiritual dunce, I tried my best to keep my head up, but it was all I could do to sit and listen to the pastor as he spoke about the power of the Holy Spirit. His words sounded so foreign to me, like he was speaking Greek and everyone else could understand him. My church background offered little to no experience with things concerning the Holy Spirit. Jesus? Sure. Father God? Of course. But the mystical, unpredictable and often misinterpreted third member of the Trinity? Uncanny silence. For my church, it was The Father, The Son, and The Holy Bible.

So as Pastor Jimmy continued talking about the power of the Holy Spirit, I got increasingly antsy, fidgeting in my seat. What I found strange, though, was the guy seemed completely normal. No three piece suit. No snakes. Just blue jeans and a button down. He wasn't just pulling thoughts out of thin air, either. He was preaching straight out of the Bible.

Then, he started telling us about what was going on all over the world. How God was moving in powerful ways, revival sweeping across South America, for example. All these people didn't sound strange at all. They sounded just like simple, humble folks hungry for more of God, crying out in prayer. He spoke of whole villages giving their lives to Jesus. Entire regions swept along in the fires of revival.

He then spoke of the move of God in China, the greatest revival in history. A hundred million people coming to Christ. Young teenagers crying out for the power of God and not only seeing the sick healed, but people raised from the dead. He spoke of Africa, how signs and wonders have become the norm among churches. Global Christianity, he explained, had become more focused in the southern hemisphere because of a massive move of the Holy Spirit. God was using just simple, ordinary people who know their weakness, but trusted in God's power.

Then, he started talking about us here in America. So often we try to put God in a box, wary of anything we might not be able to control. In regards to the gifts of the Spirit, we mostly offer a collective 'no thanks'. But if you look at the church worldwide, unprecedented growth occurs in the places where the gifts of the Holy Spirit are embraced, not stiff-armed like they are so often in the western church.

As hard as it was to admit, I knew I'd been trying to cram God into my predictable little box for as long as I could remember. I'd always tried to call the shots. And I realized at that moment that my own pride had been the very thing that sabotaged a greater move of God in my life.

Sitting on that creaky wooden pew, my heart began to pound. My stomach twisted. I grew nauseous. Face to face with my pride, my obsession with control. My fear of ever being weird had caused me to continually miss God and I knew I had to surrender my death grip on the steering wheel if I hoped to see greater fruit in my life.

I didn't want to miss what God was doing on the Earth. I didn't want to keep building my own little spiritual kingdom.

"If you want this," Jimmy said. "If you are willing to humble yourself and give God complete control, and you long for more power, more gifts, more of God, then come to the front right now."

No lie, at that moment, when those words left Jimmy's mouth, I practically leapt to my feet and raced to the front of the auditorium. I fell to my knees and started repenting for everything I could think of.

"God," I prayed, "I'm sorry for resisting You. I'm sorry for being so prideful. I'm so sorry that I've always been way more into me and my appearance and my image and my gifts than knowing my desperate need for You and Your power."

While I was still on my knees at the alter, a fiery little Asian woman walked right up to me, placed her hand on my back and started declaring, "He's a self made man, Lord. He's a self made man!"

I was trembling and weeping and feeling at any moment that lightning was about to strike me to cinders. Judgement day had fallen.

"Oh God, help me!" I cried.

Then, all of a sudden, the power of God struck me like a bolt of electricity. This had never happened to me before. Not even close. I started shaking on the ground.

Yes. Shaking.

Right then, I thought. Oh no. I'm one of the weird ones now.

The irony was beautiful.

Fiery Asian lady then leaned down close to my ear and spoke. "You're a self made man ... but if you humble yourself God will raise you up as a leader in this generation."

At these words, I melted to the ground. The tangible, manifest power of God swept over me again and again like waves upon the ocean. I didn't get up off the floor for thirty minutes. By the time I opened my eyes and rose to my feet, everyone had left the service. Well, everyone but one extremely emotional college girl weeping on the floor a few feet away from me. She was pulling herself off the carpet at the same time and gave me a knowing look.

Awkward.

"Uhmm," I said, wiping the snot from my nose. "Hi." I sheepishly walked out of the sanctuary, dazed by the experience and wondering what it all meant.

That night we returned to the streets to share the gospel and pray for the sick. It was a crowded market place, the smell of roasting meat and fried tortillas hanging in the air. Tejano music blared from unseen speakers as people milled about, in search of a bit of night life, or a good deal from one of the trinket venders along the thoroughfare. I moved amidst the crowd, searching for people to share Jesus with as I had in the park the night before. But this time, as I talked with my first person, taking them through a tract of the gospel, the result was entirely different.

"Do you want to give your life to Jesus?"

Without hesitation. "Si."

Trying to subdue my elation, I led them through a prayer and gave them a Bible.

The next person I shared with?

"Si."

Again, I prayed with them and gave them a Bible.

FOUR PEOPLE gave their lives to Christ that night as I shared the gospel. I could hardly contain myself. When it was announced over a loud speaker that we would pray for the sick, a swarm of people emerged from the crowd, upwards of two hundred people. Instantly sheepish, I stepped back to allow others to lead out in the praying. I didn't want to mess things up, so I decided to guard the bags our team had brought. At least I could serve in that way.

People were paired off in groups for prayer and I was relieved to see no one seemed to need me to pray. I could just stand there and watch—no need to make myself a total fool with ineffective intercession. Then, out of the corner of my eye, I saw an older Mexican gentleman motioning to me. I looked at him, and it was clear he wanted prayer. With instant butterflies swirling in my belly I nodded and trudged over to where he stood.

His shoulders were hunched over and he kept on pointing to his stomach. I discerned he was in a great deal of pain, both in his shoulder and stomach area. He clearly wanted prayer. Before starting, I asked another girl on our team to pray along with me. She was as naive as I was. But we both laid our hands on his stomach and started to pray, albeit timidly.

I had no idea what to pray. So I just started simple. "Jesus ... you see this man ... won't you come and heal him?"

I don't know exactly what I expected. What does God do when He heals people? But what happened next was entirely off my radar. With our hands on his stomach, his abdomen started to spasm under our palms and fingers, as if alive under his skin. That poor, sweet girl's eyes went wide with shock. Then his shoulder and back began to pop, as if cracking back into place. Now the girl was crying, and not out of worshipful awe ... but out of pure terror. Both of us were almost in shock.

What in the heck is going on?

This wasn't just weird. This was freakishly uncanny. This was paradigm shifting. This was undeniable, totally tangible stuff literally at our fingertips. The Mexican man's face went beet red as his body seemed to contort back to normal. He started to weep as he realized what had happened. And then, to our utter disbelief, he stood up perfectly straight, eyes wide, and lifted his hands high into the air, worshipping as tears streamed down his face.

"Glory a Dios," he said, a smile spreading wide across his weathered face. "Gloria a Dios! Gracias, Cristo ... Gracias!"

I called out for a translator to come over and help us figure out what had happened. When one finally joined us, the old man explained.

"For twenty years," he began, eyes bloodshot and brimming with tears, "I've been in intense pain and suffering ... and in this instant, Jesus healed me."

To this day, this remains one of the most powerful moments of my life.

I wasn't some kind of faith healer. I had no power or anointing on my own. This was straight-up the power of God. In an instant, I was ruined for the ordinary ... for the mundane.

And I've never gone back.

So, let me ask you a question: If you could have more spiritual power in your life, wouldn't you want it?

In Acts, Jesus tells His followers that when the Holy Spirit falls upon them, they will have power to reach the world. Now stop for a moment and think about this. The creator of the universe, with limitless authority and strength, gives us power. He calls us to reach the world and pours into us everything we need to see it done. For Jesus' followers, it wasn't supposed to be a 'someday I'll have impact' perspective. He didn't fill them so that years later they could reach some far off nation. He said *Jerusalem, Judea and Samaria, and to the end of the earth.*

This is synonymous with saying 'hometown, state, country, and the rest of the entire world.' God wants to fill you with the Holy Spirit in order to give you power to reach people today ... right where you are. Eventually, you might reach the four corners of the earth, but for now, He's empowered you to change your workplace, your street, and your family. Don't allow the word "someday" into your spiritual vocabulary. Ditch the word "tomorrow" as well. We never know how long we'll have on the earth. The power of God moves in the present tense. Here and now.

So what can you do?

The Bible says in Mark 12:31 to *"Love your neighbor as yourself."* This is truly the most radical thing you can do. And I don't mean some generalized group of people in your proximity. I'm talking your literal neighbor. It's so odd in America, how so many of us don't even know the names of people living right next door. Go meet those people. Strike up a friendship. Let the Holy Spirit move through you and help bring them into the Kingdom.

The power of God falls on us not just so we can move overseas and share Jesus with some Stone Age tribe. He fills us so we can reach people right across the street, just over a fence. I know this can feel awkward at first, but it's really quite simple. Let me lay out a quick strategy for "cold turkey" evangelism.

Walk up to their door. Ring the doorbell.

Now the next part is key ... pay close attention, because your choice of words here can make or break the deal. When they come to the door, smile (for starters), and then say, "Hi ... my name's Robert" (but don't tell them your name's Robert, unless your name is actually Robert).

Got that? It's a complicated business, I know, but I believe in you.

Then, if the first interchange went over well, ask, "How are you doing?"

You'd be amazed how many varied conversational topics might arise from this question.

My tongue-in-cheek point is that it's not that big of deal. Just make a friend. Bake them some cookies. Invite them over for dinner. Get into their lives and just start praying for them. In all likelihood, they've never known anyone like you before, no one to care for them so much, and probably no one to pray for them. Over time, you're sure to see their hearts soften toward

God ... perhaps even to the point of giving their lives to Jesus. All because of a simple neighbor-to-neighbor introduction.

For students: Do you know the person sitting next to you in class?

Do you know the name of the waiter at your favorite restaurant? I'm telling you, some of the most powerful gospel-sharing moments I've had came from praying for wait staff when our family goes out to eat on occasion.

You will receive power to be my witnesses.

It all starts right smack dab in front of you. But the end is beyond imagination. Never underestimate the power of God in your life. Who knows, you just might see entire nations swept up into God's story. But the journey always begins with a single step, an initial heartfelt prayer for a nation you feel strangely burdened for.

Let's close by looking at Acts chapter two.

"When the day of Pentecost came, they were all together in one place. Suddenly a sound like the blowing of a violent wind came from heaven and filled the whole house where they were sitting. They saw what seemed to be tongues of fire that separated and came to rest on each of them."

- Acts 2:1-3

Okay. That's weird. That's not normal church service activity. When you think about it, these guys would have been kicked out of most churches these days.

"I'm sorry, but we have a 'no rushing wind' policy. Not to mention the forbidding of open flames in our bylaws. We're gonna have to ask you to leave. Goodbye, and God bless."

But things got even crazier:

"All of them were filled with the Holy Spirit and began to speak in other tongues as the Spirit enabled them. Now there were staying in Jerusalem God-fearing Jews from every nation under heaven. When they heard this sound, a crowd came together in bewilderment, because each one heard their own language being spoken."
- Acts 2:4-6

The city was filled with all kinds of nationalities, and as the disciples spoke under the power of the Holy Spirit, they started to speak in different languages. Complete foreigners started hearing God's praises in their native language. The disciples got so rocked by the Holy Spirit, the crowds thought they'd had a little too much of the communion wine.

They were actually accused of being drunk.

From a logical point of view, this was not the smoothest of God's moves, at least it doesn't seem so. But the proof is in the pudding, so to speak. That very day, thousands came to Christ when Peter delivered a sermon about Jesus and the gospel.

You will receive power to be my witnesses.

Power.

To be my witnesses.

People won't come to Christ because of our eloquence. We might be the smoothest talkers around and still see nothing happen. It's when the power of God falls. When the Holy Spirit takes our weak and frail bodies and tiny little brains and carries us along into something miraculous.

When we hear about God moving all over the world, it's not because a certain group of Christians figured out the best strategy, the most effective apologetic arguments, or preached the most articulate delivery of sermons. It's the power of God. Period. It's about God moving in the midst of His followers, the light shining in the midst of darkness.

I'm well aware that certain people in the body of Christ can get weirded out by other believers aggressively pursuing the power of the Holy Spirit. But I am unapologetically suggesting that you aggressively pursue the power of the Holy Spirit. If people get offended by your hunger for more of God, so be it. Religious people have responded this way from the beginning because of a simple lack of understanding.

Make no mistake, I am fully committed to being rooted in the Word of God. And within the pages of the Bible there are healings, visions, and miracles. There are signs and wonders aplenty. While God is not a God of chaos, He is not predictable. He is good, but He does not live in a box.

But what about when it gets weird?

In truth, this happens when it becomes solely about the next church meeting. When our hunger for more is reduced to a longing for some supernatural experience, it becomes selfish. It becomes about us, rather than reaching out to others with the truth of God.

The power is for a purpose.

That purpose is presenting the nations to Jesus.

If there is something God wants to give to the Church, then for crying out loud I want it! I'd be stupid not to. If He's offering me something that will make ministry so much easier, removing the responsibility from my shoulders of winning souls, then how in the world could I possibly say 'no'? If I tried all day to fly, by flapping my arms as hard as I could, we all know that my feet would never leave the ground and I'd end up exhausted from the effort. By contrast, walking in the power of the Holy Spirit is like riding a hot air balloon. We hop in the basket and rise up into the air through no power of our own. The view's a lot better up there anyway, and a lot more fun, I assure you.

I'm not good enough, or smart enough, or strong enough to accomplish much on my own. But I have the Holy Spirit living within me. I'm simply a conduit of His presence, of His power, of His love for the world.

And that's a good reason to party.

7

A DAY TO ENJOY

When I was a kid I had a hamster named Teddy Bear. Now why anyone would waste their time and money having an over-sized rodent as a pet is beyond me, but to me as a kid, it was cute and furry, so why not?

Teddy Bear's home was a standard hamster habitat. Cedar shaving floor, water bottle, little basin for hamster food, and so on. But of all these things, his favorite was the yellow plastic hamster wheel. The little guy just loved it. He spent almost every waking hour running and running on that circular eternity.

A sad irony was that Teddy Bear was rather fat—as rodents go—and no matter how long he ran, he never lost an ounce. Maybe he had a glandular problem. Who knows? But when I think about the poor thing and its fruitless exercise, I'm reminded how so many of us view life in much the same way.

Daily drudgery. Nothing but pointless toil.

I saw a billboard the other day as I drove down the highway. In stark black letters it said, "You work ... and then you die."

Wow. Thanks, random advertiser. All of us commuters really needed your uplifting adage.

The fact is that many people think this way. Life has no point. No real, lasting enjoyment. It's stress and pain and labor and strain. Just a long string of dreary days leading to the grave.

But thank God there's more.

Hopefully this book has, so far, brought you some good news. We've talked about God's partying people and God's heart of extravagant celebration. We've talked about Jesus' love for parties and hopefully turned your 'boring church' paradigm on its head. But did you know it gets even better? Did you know that each week God wants there to be a day dedicated solely to our enjoyment and celebration?

I kid you not.

Let's jump into Genesis where God unveils this beautiful gift called the Sabbath. For some context, let me paint the picture. God has just spread the universe out on his heavenly canvas and brought the world into being. He created light from darkness, the sea and dry land, plants and animals of unimaginable variation and beauty. Everything we see and know, brought forth from His creative hand. And at the end of the sixth day, He created man in His image, the crown jewel of a masterpiece.

Let's pick up in chapter two:

"Thus the heavens and the earth were completed in their vast array. By the seventh day God had finished the work he had began doing. So on the seventh day He rested from all His work. And God blessed the seventh day and made it holy because on it He rested from all the work of creating that He had done."
- Genesis 2:1-3

Here's a little pop quiz for you: Does God need to rest?
Take as long as you need. I'll go fix some tea.

NO! He doesn't need to rest. How utterly ridiculous.

He is the epitome of strength. God is omnipotent, which is just a fancy word for all-powerful. The Bible says He neither sleeps nor slumbers, and His strength never runs out. So why did God take a divine siesta? Let me propose to you that the reason God rested is because rest is good.

Repeat those words for me: Rest is good.

It might seem a stretch for us go-getter Americans to comprehend the value and blessing of rest. But it was God's idea. And who are we to argue, despite our capitalistic genius? So, if God says it's good, then it's good. Case closed.

God created a day of rest where He actually sat back and enjoyed Himself. I love to imagine Him crossing his arms over His chest, gazing out over His creation, a contented smile lifting the corners of His mouth, then with a sigh of pure satisfaction saying, *"Ahhhh, would you just look at that? Lovely."*

Now let's look at it from man's perspective. Remember, man was created on the sixth day. He's hardly dusted the dirt from his newly created skin, with lungs breathing Eden air for only a few hours. Surely the guy was like a kid bursting through the gates of Disney World for the first time.

"Wow, God! Look at all this stuff!" he must have wanted to say. "Let's go name all these animals ... let's go climb that mountain over there. Let's pick some fruit and chase a lion. There's just so much to *do!*"

But God's like, *Nope. Today, on your first full day on the earth, you know what we're gonna do? Rest.*

Man hasn't even done anything yet. Hardly a muscle twitch of exertion and no accomplishments to speak of, and God tells him to take a load off. Sounds a bit inefficient if you ask me. Seems like God should have worked him at least a little bit before giving him a vacation day. Maybe name the marsupials first or something. But no. He gave Adam a break before he broke a single drop of sweat.

This, I believe, is enormously important to understand in our walk with God.

The beginning of our faith comes from rest.

Adam didn't create a thing, but he was granted rest from the start. Similarly, we did not do a single solitary thing to earn our salvation. God grants it as a gift, sending His son to earth to live and die for us in order to pay the price for our sins. Grace. Mercy. Love. All a gift from God ... to be believed, received, and enjoyed. We do not strive to earn God's love. We rest in it as sure as a child does his own father's love.

We rest in the finished work of the cross.

That's what we see from the very beginning of scripture.

Rest is the starting point.

If we get this, ladies and gentlemen, if we really allow it to seep into our bones of belief, our lives are going to be infinitely more enjoyable. We will enter into the abundant life God has called us to.

There are three components of the Sabbath that God invites us to enter into. As we read in the beginning of Genesis chapter two, God finished His work then rested on the seventh day, blessing it and making it holy.

God rested. He blessed it. He made it holy.

Sabbath is not just something we need to know about, like some Sunday-school construct. He wants us to experience it. To walk into its blessing. So let's break it down.

He rested.

I often wonder what kind of old man I will be. What am I going to be like when I'm in my eighties or nineties? Will I be a crusty old curmudgeon leaning on a cane with a scowl frozen on my face, grumpy as all get out? Or will I be a man still full of joy and vigor, ever smiling in the final years of my life? Will I have followed God's lead and allowed myself enough rest to stay balanced through the years, loving God to the end, a shining light all the way to my last breath?

I was talking with one of my mentors recently about a time in his mid life when he had a significant physical breakdown. This guy loves Jesus like crazy and has lived radically for the Kingdom for decades. He didn't freak out and buy a Porsche or anything. He just kind of hit the wall physically. His body just seemed to break down. His energy reserves, once virtually limitless, had been reduced to fumes. Seeking answers, he made a call to one of the foremost authorities on adrenaline and stress here in California.

During their counseling sessions the doctor told him that many of the problems he had faced could have been rectified if he'd rested properly.

We need rest.

What happens when we don't rest? Think about it. Our bodies start to feel run down. We become more susceptible to sickness and disease. Our brains get all cloudy and sluggish. Our brains seem to turn to sludge when we don't give them a chance to switch off for a bit. We get cranky. Easily upset. No one really likes to be around a person who hasn't slept in a while, kind of like a snake coiled in a corner, ready to strike.

Historically, rest has often been disregarded. I read about a time during the industrial revolution when the nation of France, in order to boost productivity, mandated a seven-day workweek.

Eventually, without a day off, things started going badly. Horses started dying from exhaustion. Sickness among people grew rampant. Crime rates skyrocketed. Soon people noticed that factories were much more productive if workers were allowed a day of rest.

In World War II, when the demand for ships grew, the US government required a seven-day workweek for its contracted businesses. There was a man named Walter Mellon who was the founder and CEO of Correct Craft, one of the primary ship building companies at the time. He was a strong believer and refused the requirement, citing the Bible's command for a day of rest. With the government threatening to pull his contract he asked for a chance to demonstrate how his six-day policy could prove more productive. The government agreed and Correct Craft went on to perform far and above its competitors on all fronts.

We were made for maximum efficiency only when we take time to rest.

The beautifully ironic thing about the whole business is that it actually takes more faith to rest than to work all the time.

Ponder this: Do you think God was finished with His work when He rested?

Of course not. Creation didn't end on the sixth day. He's been working ever since, moving in peoples' lives, continually breathing life into the universe. But God realized that after the sixth day, the fitting thing to do was take a day of rest. He instituted the Sabbath for us. As a model. A demonstration of His perfect plan.

When you enter into rest, you imitate our righteous God. With the obedience of rest, it's like you're saying, "God, I trust You. I'm taking one day a week and choosing not to work, and I'm trusting You to make up for my lack." That project might not be finished. You may need to earn more money. But take a day of rest anyway and watch God work on your behalf. It's so much more fun that way when you think about it.

For me personally, it's been a challenge at times to willfully rest. I'm an action-oriented person. I like to be going. I like to be moving. I like to be checking my iPhone for news and stats and whatever. So it takes a good bit of discipline for me to stop dead in my tracks and choose rest. It takes faith to pause and let the world turn on without me, allowing God to work on my behalf. Each day I choose to rest, I remind myself that God can do in one day what I could not possibly accomplish in seven. I loosen my hands from the handlebars. I un-grit my teeth. And just sit back and watch.

He blessed it.

When the Sabbath was first instituted there was a religious group called the Pharisees. These guys were Sabbatarians, which means that they got really into the Sabbath. I mean really. They were self-proclaimed, self-appointed experts and made it their obsession to define a code of conduct for such a holy day. Not only that, they decided to take the entire principle and force it on everyone by making it law.

Sometimes, as religious people, we can do this very thing. We hear something good, some rich truth, and then assume it's our job to force it on everyone else. We evaluate and judge and assess people's levels of righteousness based on how well they perform in our eyes. If folks don't do what we deem holy to perfection, they're losers.

The Pharisees got so into the law of the Sabbath they eventually felt dissatisfied with how God had defined it. He didn't specify enough. The concept of rest was too vague. People needed some good old-fashioned guardrails to keep them on the straight and narrow. "They're all just dumb sheep anyway," the Pharisees thought. "They aren't as holy as we are so let's give them a little help."

What followed was the creation of some of the most ludicrous rules imaginable.

Here are some examples just for fun:

You weren't supposed to carry a burden on the Sabbath, but the Pharisees wanted to clearly define what a "burden" was. They got together, debated, argued, and finally came to the conclusion that a burden constituted anything heavier than a dried fig. Wow. Way to go guys. So helpful.

So, if a candle melts and wax gets on the ground, you can't pick it up and move the wax. If a horse sheds a hair, you can't pick up the hair. You can't even carry a piece of paper. If your hen lays an egg on the Sabbath, you can't eat it, because your hen was working. How dare that unholy chicken! The Pharisees said you couldn't even move your clothing around on the Sabbath. Even if your house was on fire, all that you were allowed to do was escape with the clothes on your back. As a result, people would throw on extra layers as flames rose up around them just so they could stay obedient to the Sabbath code before fleeing for their lives. Geez.

When Jesus came along, He didn't abolish the Sabbath. He came to fulfill the law. But let's look at what He had to say about God's day of rest.

"At that time Jesus went through the grainfields on the Sabbath. His disciples were hungry and began to pick some heads of grain and eat them. When the Pharisees saw this, they said to Him, 'Look, your disciples are doing what's unlawful on the Sabbath.' He answered them, 'Haven't you read what David did when he and his companions were hungry? He entered the house of God, and he and his companions ate the consecrated bread—which was not lawful for them to do, but only for the priests. Or haven't you read in the Law that the priests on Sabbath duty in the temple desecrate the Sabbath and yet are innocent? I tell you that something greater than the Temple is here. If you had known what these words mean,

"I desire mercy, not sacrifice," you would not have condemned the innocent. For the Son of Man is Lord of the Sabbath."'
- Matthew 12:1-8

Jesus didn't mince words here. I love it. He's saying 'Look guys, these people are hungry ... and I like to let them have some grain if they need to eat. They're just walking through the field picking granola off the stalks. Relax, already! Don't condemn them. I'm here to bless them! I'm the Lord of the Sabbath for crying out loud!'

But the plot thickens further.

"Going on from that place He went to their synagogue, and a man with a shriveled hand was there. Looking for a reason to bring charges against Jesus, they asked Him, 'Is it lawful to heal on the Sabbath?' He said to them, 'If any of you has a sheep and it falls into a pit on the Sabbath, will you not take hold of it and lift it out? How much more valuable is a man than a sheep? Therefore, it's lawful to do good on the Sabbath.' Then He said to the man, 'Stretch out your hand.' So he stretched it out and it was completely restored, just as sound as the other."
- Matthew 12:9-13

This is such an awesome picture of Jesus blessing people on the Sabbath. If the first component of the Sabbath is rest, the second is blessing. Jesus says it's not about heaping laws on people, it's about His desire to bless.

In Mark chapter two, the same story of Jesus' disciples eating grain appears again. Jesus said, 'The Sabbath was made for man, not man for the Sabbath.' God instituted the Sabbath because He loves us and He wants to bless us.

One of my favorite icebreaker questions when I'm in a small group setting is this: "If you had a free day, a day where you could do whatever you wanted. What would you do?" I love it because every time I ask this question you can hear an audible sigh in the room. People can't help but smile and get a wistful, far off look.

"I'd take a walk on a beach," some would say.

"I'd just curl up by the fire with a good book and a hot cup of tea," others might answer.

People love thinking about this because it's like daydreaming. We hardly ever get to actually do these kind of things. But did you know that God wants you to have times of enjoyment and delight? He loves it when you enjoy His creation. When you delight in the good gifts He has given. The Bible says that *"Every good and perfect gift comes down from above, from the Father of lights where there is no shadow of turning."* (James 1:17) God loves to give good gifts. He is a God of delight, not just some kind of task-master. He doesn't sit up in heaven with His nose to the grindstone, demanding that we get to work, get to work, get to work! We see evidence of this in creation itself. We see God's playfulness.

How many colors do we actually need in order to function on the earth? It would have been so simple and so easy to just have a few essential hues. Black, white, gray ... maybe tan. But God created so many colorful variations we can scarcely label them all. Think about how many shades of blue there are! Dark blue, navy blue, light blue, turquoise, aqua, neon blue and likely thousands more. Just blue, people! Take into account the rest of the color spectrum and your mind might get blown. Have you ever scuba dived in a coral reef? Me neither. But I've seen video. God was having a little creation party when He made coral reefs. He was probably smiling from ear to ear, shaking His wizened head in delight as He dabbed color after color and shape after shape.

We could have just had roses. But instead we have roses and daisies and daffodils and countless other flowers in variations all over the world. There's even a kind of orchid in the rain forest whose scent smells exactly like rotten meat. It's so bad it draws clouds of flies that end up pollinating the flowers as they land from blossom to blossom. That's just freaky, like God wanted to throw things for a loop. And what about flowers that no one will ever see, blooming in a cleft of some rock high up on a mountain? To me, this is undeniable evidence of God's playfulness.

And what about the animals? We could have just had a few standard species—lions and tigers and bears (oh my). But instead we have the mind-bending presence of the duckbill platypus. I mean, come on! It lays eggs, but's it's a mammal. It has a beak, but no feathers. God must have a sense of humor. What about the okopi? Is it a zebra or a giraffe? And flying squirrels? Do squirrels really need to fly? Probably not. But God made them anyway, just for the fun of it. Just to be enjoyed.

God invites us into this same delight.

The Sabbath is a day to enjoy. A day to savor what God has done.

I was recently talking to a theological mentor of mine, Father David J. Montzingo, a spirit-filled Episcopalian priest who is a real scholar in matters of faith. We were discussing this idea of being blessed on the Sabbath.

He took me into the word recreation, which, if you split it apart, becomes re and create. Drawing from the original Latin roots, re means to do again while create means to establish, or invigorate. Have you ever done an activity that just makes you come alive? Whenever you get the chance to take part in it you feel your spirit rising, a visceral pleasure. For some of us it's reading a good book. For others it's hopping on a ten speed bike and going for a long ride. For some of you, it's playing dominos. Seriously. I know people like this. For some it's painting. For some it's cooking. You just love crafting dishes from scratch and hovering over a flaming stove. (This is not me, but to each his own. I'll take pleasure in eating whatever you make.)

For me, it's being out in nature. Going on a long hike. This last Sabbath, we borrowed some kayaks and my son Hudson and I were out on Mission Bay just as the sun was setting. The water was like glass. Heaven on earth, folks. My son wanted to race, digging his paddle in the water, but I said, "No, son ... let's just savor the moment." I was alive ... breathing the dusky air with my son at my side and the water reflecting the sunset like a million blazing mirrors.

We can do things that re-create us into the person God wants us to be.

God took six days to create and then one day to be refreshed and blessed. When He saw all He had done He sat back and said, 'It is good.' And as His children, we've got to do the same. We need to take a break. To get off the treadmill of our lives, look around at God's limitless blessing, and say 'It is GOOD! I'm going to enjoy God's blessing!'

I'm giving you official permission, right here and now, to do things you delight in. I'm giving you permission, for what it's worth, to rest. Some people grew up with an entirely different paradigm. In your home, rest might have seemed like laziness. I met a girl the other day who said her parents always told her that 'idol hands are the Devil's tool.' Like if you rest, you're going to get possessed or something. You chill out for a moment, and all of a sudden the Devil's inside you. Whatever!

What about this lie: If I rest a while, then I'm not advancing the Kingdom.

Objection, your Honor! If you rest, you are imitating God ... allowing Him the chance to refresh, reinvigorate, and reestablish you in His strength so that when you get back out in His service again, you are even more effective than before.

Objection sustained.

When you rest, you end up with more power and more love and more vision ... ultimately, more light. And the world needs to see this light. The Bible says, *"Taste and see that the Lord is GOOD."* If all you do is labor and toil and strive without taking the time to rest and enjoy God, then all the world will see is a slave bent under the heavy hand of a task master. Why in the world would they want to follow such a God? You're too depressed to be around anyway, killjoy!

Learn to rejoice in God's goodness. It's like a mile long buffet where each dish gets better than the last. And the more we linger there, the more refreshed we become. This is exciting stuff! I'm about ready to have a Sabbath right here and now.

He made it holy.

There are many ways to make something holy but the first that comes to mind is what the people of God did for centuries on the Sabbath: worship.

Exodus 20:8 says, 'Remember the Sabbath day by keeping it holy.'

This was so important that God included it in the Ten Commandments. Often we can resist laws, feeling they restrict us with heavy burdens, but I'm here to tell you that God's law was given to bring life—to bring blessing. It's a good thing we were told not to kill each other and rob each other blind. I tend to thank God for things that keep me alive and with my shirt. Keeping the Sabbath day is right in there with 'Don't murder.' Is it just me, or does this carry a certain weight of importance? Maybe we should listen to what God's saying here?

Remember the Sabbath and keep it holy. Why? Because God wants us to enter into His blessing. Over and over, scripture describes people bringing offerings to God on the Sabbath, gathering at the temple to hear the Word of the Lord. We see God's people in a rhythm of worship and prayer, setting aside one day a week to seek Him. Jesus went into the synagogue to teach people on the Sabbath. And then later the apostles Peter and Paul regularly entered the synagogue, as was their custom on the Sabbath, to teach the people God's Word. Throughout history, folks have gathered weekly as the people of Christ to pray and grow in their knowledge of God.

I am so thankful that my parents established this routine in our family growing up. We didn't have a vibrant church. It was more akin to the 'frozen chosen.' But my parents taught me that once a week we were to gather with the people of God at church. And it was there, even as a kid and into my teenage years, that I began to learn about the Word of God. I developed a community with the people of God. And I learned to love the simple act of singing worship songs to God. Even then, I was experiencing God's presence.

Now, as I look back, I'm so blessed my parents were committed to church, even though I resisted from time to time. Some Sundays I'd beg them to let me stay home so I could watch the Lone Ranger on TV, even though it was in black and white. I just wanted to watch the guy running around with Tonto, on his white horse and wearing his black mask, saving the day instead of fidgeting on a boring pew for two hours. But every time, my attempts at persuasion were met with kind but firm denial. My friends would be going to the lake to hang out for the day, but I'd always have to dress up and go to church. At the time, it felt like agony. But now, years later, I see the value of my parents' commitment.

I look at my parents now, in their fortieth year of a wonderful marriage. And I consider my sisters and myself: all of us have given our lives to Christ. All of us have healthy marriages. There are ten grandkids running around. Everyone is following God and trying to advance His Kingdom. I attribute a lot of this fruit to the way my parents led our family back in the day. We had a nonnegotiable value of once a week gathering with the people of God, just like it's been done for centuries, worshiping Christ and growing in the truth of His Word.

This changes you.

It leaves an indelible mark.

Gathering with the people of God is integral to our growth as followers of Jesus.

Hebrews 10:24 says, *"And let us consider how we may spur one another on toward love and good deeds."*

Have you ever met anyone who says, "I don't really want to be more loving. I'm as loving as I need to be."

For me, I'm like, "PLEASE MAKE ME MORE LOVING! Especially to my kids!" I'm desperate for more spiritual fruit in my life. If gathering with other believers on a consistent basis will help me grow, then of course I'm all for it. Now, I pastor a church, so it's natural for me to want people to attend, but even if I flipped burgers for a living I'd be busting down the doors of church every Sunday morning because I know that's where the party is. I know it's a place that will help me grow. The world is desperate to see people who express the heart of God, who shine their light in the darkness like a torch. When we gather together as believers, it's like feeding the flame.

Hebrews 10:25 goes on to say, *"… not giving up meeting together, as some are in the habit of doing, but encouraging one another - and all the more as you see the Day approaching."*

When we come together, it's to be a place of encouragement. And who doesn't want to be encouraged? We all get weary. We all get tired. Meeting with the people of God can be like a well-needed salve.

So let me sum it up: the Sabbath equips us to be the people God has called us to be. As we come together as God's family, feeding on the Word of God, encountering His presence, and connecting with others, we are recalibrated for the week ahead.

Before ending this chapter, let me answer a few questions I know are pretty common among believers regarding the Sabbath.

1) Was there a particular day denoted as the Sabbath in scripture?

For the Jews it was designated as Saturday. That was their seventh day of the week. For most Christians, Sunday is believed to be the true Sabbath day. The reasoning behind this choice was derived from Mark 2:27-88 and Luke 6:5-6, where Jesus actually says the Son of Man is the Lord of the Sabbath. The Sabbath day was moved to Sunday on account of His rising from the grave on that day. Revelation chapter one paints this picture as well—the Apostle John writes, *"On the Lord's day I was in the spirit ... "*

Another angle can be found in Romans 14.

"One person considers one day more sacred than another; another considers every day alike. Each of them should be fully convinced in their own mind. Whoever regards one day as special does so to the Lord. Whoever eats meat does so to the Lord, for they give thanks to God; and whoever abstains does so to the Lord and gives thanks to God."
- Romans 14:5-6

Here's the main point: It's not about entering back into rules and regulations. It's about having a Sabbath lifestyle. It's about living a life where we say, "One day a week I'm going to try to downshift, to rest, to enter into God's blessing and come and worship Him."

It's not about this day or that day, but a lifestyle.

2) If Sunday is a Sabbath for most Christians, should I not work on Sunday?

I remember as a kid growing up, it seemed all the shops were closed on Sunday. Let me assure you, there was a time when most establishments shut their doors on the Sabbath. Chik-Fil-A and Hobby Lobby are still closed on Sunday, and they seem to be doing pretty well for themselves. Go figure.

As far as personal work goes—I consider it a reasonable and wise idea to take a day of rest. But there are some obvious exceptions. Just think about hospitals. I'm really glad medical personnel don't lock up the doors and leave the rest of us to fend for ourselves if we get sick. I might be able to set a bone if my kid breaks an arm, but I couldn't for the life of me perform an appendectomy. At least not without making a big mess of it. And what about police officers? What if all the cops said 'Peace out!' on Sunday? There would be a crime spree every Sabbath for sure. Can you imagine? Getting home from church and sitting down to a nice lunch of fried chicken and mashed potatoes while criminals roam the street unrestrained? No thank you. And what about firemen? Fires don't take a day off, so I'm grateful firefighters don't check out every Sunday and leave us to fight our little infernos with garden hoses or water guns.

But, please allow me to be bold. I am compelled to address the issue of our materialistic society. These days, the retail machine cranks at full speed on Sunday. People shop it up like no one's business. But let me ask you, is our country better off because we can go out and buy anything we want on Sunday? Has this gotten us anywhere? Do you feel closer with your family because of it? Has it improved our standard of living? Has it made life more enjoyable? Or made us more godly? This is not a legalistic thing by any means. I'm just trying to make a point. Some of us never get to stop because Sunday has just become another day in the rat race.

So, here's my challenge today: If you can ... if you have a choice for a day off (which most people do), pick Sunday. Why? Well, because it's the day people of God around the whole world are coming together to worship. It's also a weekend and will offer the best chance for longer spans of rest and enjoyment. Take the time necessary to rest at the end of the week. Take the time to dine. Enjoy life with your friends and family. We were hardwired by God to pause from our labor, to rest, taste, and see that the Lord is good.

Choosing a midweek day for a Sabbath could prove a challenge for many because the temptation to keep cranking on work can be pretty strong. Everyone else would be working and thus, there wouldn't be much time to celebrate anyway. At least not with others. That's why I believe Sunday is the best day—others are more likely to be on the same page. Your family and friends will be ready to worship and rest right along with you.

For me, as a pastor, I can't take Sundays off. Ironic, I know. But I'm off to work very early to get things ready for our services. And oftentimes, I'm one of the last people to get home after church is over. Sunday, more often than not, is a pretty long and grueling day. I have to choose another day as a Sabbath. So, obviously I'm not mandating Sunday for anyone. The main challenge for me is just to take Sabbath. Don't neglect the blessing or you might end up a dried up sliver of beef jerky in need of a long, long nap.

3) I'm a parent, and I love Sabbath ... but I can't seem to get my kids to stop eating and needing me 24/7.

My wife and I have four kids born pretty close together. At one point our house was literally crawling with babies. Diaper after diaper after diaper ... spit up and feeding ... choking hazards. It was a full court press there for a little while. Taking a break would have been disastrous. So how in the world can we take Sabbath as parents of young kids?

Here's the deal. It's not about perfection. It's not about getting everything just how we want it. We'll probably never get there. Sabbath is an attitude of the heart. It's choosing a day where you don't rev up the engine. Moms, it's not a day where you decide to oversee Pinterest-worthy crafts or bake seven dozen snicker doodles. Relax. Downshift into first gear and forget about the mounds of laundry you have to do. Maybe when the kids are napping it's a perfect time for you to chill out with a book, or put on some music and light some candles. Whatever soothes you. My wife and I often split the duties into 'shifts'. Sometimes I'll go off on a hike while she holds down the fort and when I get back she goes out and grabs coffee with a friend.

We're even training our kids to have the same mindset. We help them get their homework done during the week so that on Sunday, when we get back from church, they're able to play in the backyard and enjoy their friends instead to sticking their noses in books and papers the rest of the day.

4) Won't I become religious and legalistic if I start following the Sabbath?

People in the church get so freaked out about this sometimes. They're so paranoid about smelling like Pharisees they flee rules like the plague. Easy, tigers. No need to panic. Let me answer this question with a question: If I had a weekly date night with my wife, where we went out and ate a nice meal together, and just enjoyed each other's company, would you point a stiff finger at my face and say, "Robert, you are soooo religious in your marriage. So legalistic with your date nights." Of course not! You'd probably admire our commitment to growing in our relationship. What if I took time weekly to play with my kids. Would you accuse me of being too rigid and dogmatic in my fatherly commitments? I certainly hope not. No! You'd want to do the same with your kids, because being a dad is one of the most rewarding adventures in life.

This is how we need to see the Sabbath. It's not some yoke God is pressing down on our shoulders. We don't do it to prove something to God. If you start doing Sabbath to earn God's favor, you're missing the whole point! You already have His love and acceptance. Jesus said, *"Come to me, all you who are weary and burdened and I will give you rest. Take my yoke upon you and learn from me, for I am gentle and humble in heart, and you will find rest for your souls. For my yoke is easy and my burden is light."* (Matthew 11:28-29)

This is what the Sabbath is all about.

Now go and enjoy yourself.

8

WHEN IT'S HARD TO PARTY

Twelve years ago, when my wife Stefanie and I had just gotten married, something happened that rendered me rather party-averse. Since we'd met and married in Texas, Stef wanted me to visit her hometown of Chicago so I could meet some of her family and friends for the first time. A wedding invitation offered the perfect opportunity for me to do just that. So, we packed up and flew to the windy city.

Now, if you knew me, you'd know full well that I never like to be underdressed for special occasions. It's something my Mom ingrained in my social paradigm. *It's better to go overdressed than underdressed since you can always peel off layers.* But being from Texas and going to college at Baylor University, my experience at weddings was that they weren't very formal. If you really want to get dressed up you put on slacks and a button-down. You were dressed to the nines if you ventured to wear a tie. So as I packed for the wedding up in Chicago I thought, *better safe than sorry.* I not only planned to wear khakis. I not only brought a tie. But I decided to bust out the best of my duds and bring along a navy blue sports jacket to boot.

I was ready to go.

From the moment we arrived at the wedding I realized something was wrong. Stefanie's mom and sister showed up in sparkling evening gowns, her brother and father trailing close behind in sleek suits. Oh no, I thought to myself. This is not good. The next moment I spotted a group of older men walking around in tuxedoes. They seem kind of old to be groomsmen, I wondered. To my horror, I soon discovered they were regular guests and it was actually a black tie wedding.

After sitting through the entire ceremony, slinking low in my seat, hoping no one would notice my profound wardrobe faux pas, I joined the eager throng as we made our way to the Exmoor Country Club across town. I've told you about the phenomenal Hotel De Coronado in San Diego ... well the Exmoor is not too far behind. Sprawled out on the emerald lawn, the guests mingled with their cocktails and hors d'oeuvres. It looked like a movie. Seriously. And there I was in my Walmart khakis, blue blazer, checked shirt, and tie. My eyes scanned the crowd for anyone ... anyone with the same level of "formal" as me. But I was awash in a sea of tuxedos and evening dresses. I felt utterly alone. The only other guest with slacks and a sport coat was a four-year old boy.

One by one Stefanie's friends approached me, each of them gliding on a film of elegance to say hello. I smiled and shook hands but every time I opened my mouth I sounded like a total hick. I've always prided myself on having a rather neutral accent, but being from Texas, my inner bumpkin can sometimes seep out.

This was such an occasion.

"Hey ya'll ... I'm Robert ... how ya doin?" I said over and over, blushing at my drawl. Never in my life had I felt more backward, and in front of all my wife's stately acquaintances.

"Where in the world did she get this guy?" I imagined them thinking.

I just wanted to fade into the background. I didn't care about the food or the dancing or even meeting my wife's family and friends. I ended up missing out because I was so self-conscious.

Now, I might be making a mountain out of a molehill with this clothing catastrophe, but I'm certain there are many people out there today who respond similarly when we talk about the partying God. You might find yourself simply too distracted by self—your own issues, your own trials—to enjoy the Kingdom celebration. Let me just say, the lie Satan wants you to believe is that if you're a Christian, and you don't feel like partying today, something is wrong with you.

It's not true.

It's a lie.

Let's jump into a story from the Bible that might shed a bit of light on the matter.

We find it in the book of John, chapter eleven, and it's centered on a particular family who knew Jesus well. So well, in fact, they partied with the Guy. (That's 'Guy' with a capital 'G'.) But in this chapter we find them facing an incredibly difficult trial.

"Now a man named Lazarus was sick. He was from Bethany, the village of Mary and her sister Martha. (This Mary whose brother now lay sick was the same Mary who poured perfume on the Lord and wiped His feet with her hair.) So the sisters sent word to Jesus, saying 'Lord, the one who you love is sick.'"
- John 11:1-3

Now, let's stop here. It's safe to say that one of the main reasons we find it hard to join in God's party is because of challenging circumstances. Somewhere in our history we bought into the notion that if we walked faithfully with God, we'd be spared pain or difficulty. But let's face it folks. Not true. Bad things happen, from tiny to tragic. Our fragile semblance of control is so often blown apart like so many leaves in a storm. It's not fun for anybody. And I'm not just talking about the bigger problems of life. Even the seemingly little stuff. The hurtful word from a friend. The annoyance of coming down with a sickness.

Let me say right here and now that I am a terrible sick person. You've seen those romantic comedies where the girl has a cold and she's all sniffly and cute in a robe under the blankets. That's not me. When my system is assaulted with an alien force of bacteria, I morph into a runny nosed tyrant. I gobble up bucketloads of medicine. I go through boxes of Kleenex. I let everyone around me know how miserable I am.

In my life I've experienced a good deal of physical affliction. Not just some old sniffly cold. As a kid I had a serious heart condition that put me in the hospital for weeks at a time. I know what it's like to feel like a victim of your own condition. The last thing you want to do is celebrate. Partying almost feels like mockery, lying on a hospital bed surrounded by flowers and cards while you've got an I.V. in your arm and are staring down at a plate of gelatinous meat loaf and flavorless green beans. I shiver at the thought.

So Lazarus was sick, this friend of Jesus. He was described by his sisters as 'the one Jesus loved.' Often we think that the closer you get to Jesus, as I said before, the fewer bad things happen to you, the more sickness fades away. Now, though I believe wholeheartedly in the healing power of God and have seen people get healed with my own eyes, I also know that steadfast followers of Jesus get sick *all the time.*

So let's do away with this little Biblical misunderstanding right here and now. We get sick. It doesn't mean God is mad and zapping us with a virus. He's right there with us in the pain. The enemy loves to mess with our minds on this issue. The moment something bad happens to us, he attacks us with thoughts like, "See! God doesn't love you. Look at all the stuff that's happening! If only you were a better person. Maybe if you prayed more and memorized more scripture you wouldn't have gotten sick." Good grief, the accuser never plays fair, does he? He's nasty.

God wants us to know His love cannot be diminished. And our trials are not innately tethered to our performance. Got it? Good. Now let's move on.

"When He heard this He said, 'The sickness will not end in death. No, it's for God's glory, so that God's Son may be glorified through it.'"
- John 11:4

Let's face it, folks: We're going to have trials in life. Period. Case closed. Pain is as guaranteed as the sunrise in the morning, like it or not. According to John 16:33, *"In this world you will have trouble."* If Jesus said it, who are we to argue? But in the midst of it we can know that God is still loving and merciful and that, in fact, He's working out our troubles for our good.

"Now Jesus loved Martha and her sister and Lazarus."
- John 11:5

Let's look at the Greek translation of the word 'love.' This particular use of the word is not just 'God loves you because you're His kid.' We often think God is obligated to love us because He created us. In this verse it actually means Jesus was fond of them. He liked them. He dearly loved these people. Yet, they found themselves in a harrowing trial. The next verse in the story is one of the most frustrating in the entire Bible.

"So when He heard that Lazarus was sick He stayed where He was for two more days."
- John 11:6

What?

A dear friend of Jesus was on his deathbed in the next town and Jesus didn't swoop in to the rescue? What's the deal? Seems like such an open-and-shut case. But Jesus doesn't do a thing about it but loiter.

We come to God so frantic and desperate sometimes, spewing out our demands like He's some kind of divine short order cook waiting for requests. "God ... You HAVE to fix things by THIS FRIDAY or I'm totally up a creek. I don't know what I'm gonna do if you don't do exactly what I'm asking."

Thursday comes and you're still freaking out, stomach tied in knots. Then Friday rolls around and NOTHING HAPPENS. "Okay God," you say. "Maybe you didn't hear me. You still have a chance to make things right. I'll give you till Sunday."

Sunday rolls around and still NOTHING. NADA. ZILCH.

"I guess there's no hope," you say, crumbling into a miserable snotty heap on the floor. "God won't help me. I am utterly alone."

Like I said, when I was twelve I developed a life threatening heart condition. For months at a time, I laid around in a hospital room. Everything seemed like it was falling to pieces. I often thought I was on my deathbed. I couldn't breathe. Once the doctors even had to pull out the defibrillators and shock me, unsure if I was going to make it. Needless to say, I was not at peace at that moment.

"COME ON, GOD!" I cried toward heaven "You've GOT to change this circumstance." But instead of getting better, I got even worse. Then, in the midst of the chaos, I got word that my granddaddy had died, a man I adored and had spent much of my childhood with. "WHAT IS GOING ON???" I prayed even harder. "I KNOW you can do something here. God ... WHY AREN'T YOU ANSWERING ME?"

You've got to know Mary and Martha and even Lazarus were thinking something similar as his sickness grew worse by the hour. Meanwhile, Jesus was talking to His disciples in the next town.

"Jesus said to His disciples, 'Let us go back to Judea.' 'But Rabbi,' they said. 'The Jews there tried to stone you. And yet you're going back?' Jesus answered, 'Are there not twelve hours of daylight? Anyone who walks in the daytime will not stumble, for they see by the world's light. It is when a person walks at night that they stumble, for they have no light.'"
- John 11:7-10

We often think God doesn't understand our problems. That he doesn't understand what it's like to be us. But when we look a little closer at this verse, we see Jesus was actually willing to walk right back into trials to help His friend. There were folks waiting to kill Him, but He didn't care. He went wherever the Father led.

Jesus is our model.

He faced trials because He knew who was with Him.

Let's continue the story.

"After He had said this He went on to tell them, 'Our friend Lazarus has fallen asleep. But I'm going there to wake him up.' His disciples replied, 'Lord, if he falls asleep he'll get better.'"
- John 11:11-12

Jesus was speaking metaphorically here. Trying to paint a little poetry into the situation. But the disciples were a little slow on the uptake.

"Now, Jesus (read this in the most moronic hick tone you can manage) ... don't go waking him up and stuff ... cuz ... uuh-hhh ... he'll need his rest." I wonder if Jesus rolled his eyes at that moment.

"Now Jesus spoke of his death, but they thought that he meant taking rest in sleep. Then Jesus told them plainly, 'Lazarus has died.'"
- *John 11:13-14*

Jesus is a realist, people! I love it. He was totally okay with talking about reality ... stark and harsh as it could be. In certain church circles, believers can be so paranoid about speaking out about something negative. Some guy could be coughing up a lung, and he'd go on smiling and insisting he wasn't sick.

It's okay to be real, in whatever situation you face. Things are hard sometimes. You don't have to wear this happy clown face when you're going through the hardest time of your life. We don't put our faith into an equation of behavior. We put our faith in God.

What Jesus says next is so incredibly interesting.

"And for your sake I'm glad I was not there so that you may believe. But let us go to him."
- *John 11:15*

We may have trials. We may have pain. But God is there in the midst of the fray, working out a plan for our good. We assume God should demonstrate His love for us by keeping us from difficulty, but He turns the notion inside out and shows us His great love by using our pain for our benefit.

I remember seeing this principle illustrated in the lives of some folks from my hometown. Larry and Nancy Madsen were close family friends, and though they were very nice people, they weren't Christians, and enjoyed a typical party lifestyle. They had two kids and were living the American dream. Everything seemed to be going great for them.

That is, until their oldest son Clay got sick.

He was a junior in high school when he was stricken with a very aggressive cancer. The family was brought to a screeching halt. In the midst of their trial, a local community of Christians surrounded them and ministered to their needs. Through this tangible display of God's love, Clay gave his life to Jesus. Soon afterwards his father did the same, and in quick succession the rest of his family followed. In the middle of tremendous pain, they found Jesus.

Sadly, the cancer continued to progress. In an effort to seek healing, the Madsens started visiting different places across the country where God was moving. I remember Larry telling me a story about going to some barn in rural Texas where an old farmer was leading worship services and praying for the sick. They joined hundreds of others crammed into the weathered wood structure, and waited for prayer. Larry had blown out his knee playing football some years prior, causing him to limp around in pain. When the old farmer started praying for him, Larry's whole body started shaking under the power of God. All of a sudden he started doing knee bends without an ounce of pain, totally and completely healed. For an hour straight, Larry bounced up and down in delight. His son Clay was touched by the power of God as well.

But he didn't get healed.

The family was saved, struck by the power of God, and full of the Holy Spirit.

But things continued to get worse in Clay's body.

"Then Thomas, also known as Didymus, said to the rest of the disciples, 'Let us also go that we might die with him.' On his arrival Jesus found out that Lazarus had already been in the tomb for four days. Now Bethany was less than two miles from Jerusalem and many Jews had come to Martha and Mary to comfort them in the loss of their brother. When Martha heard that Jesus was coming she went out to meet Him but Mary stayed at home. 'Lord,' Martha said to Jesus. 'If You had been here my brother wouldn't have died. But I know even now that God will give You whatever You ask.'"

- John 11:16-22

I think another reason people find it hard to maintain an attitude of celebration is because they don't get the answers to prayer that they wanted. Martha had surely been praying like crazy, crying out to God for healing and help. But what happened? Lazarus died anyway. So when Jesus stood before her she couldn't help but rebuke Him a little. I can just hear the strained emotion in her voice. "Lord, if you had been here, my brother would not have died."

Talk about a guilt trip! But I actually love this about her. Martha doesn't mince words. She goes boldly to Jesus and straight up speaks her mind, lobbing her question at Him without restraint. Often, in our journey of faith, our desire to reverence God precludes honest interaction. We believe we can't really go to God with our questions, or speak to Him from the depth of our souls, especially when we feel too raw in our emotions. But Martha didn't give such notions a millisecond of consideration.

If we speak honestly to God, even load Him down with

questions, this does not dishonor Him. He can handle it. David spoke honestly with God all the time. Just read the Psalms. God doesn't want a bunch of even-keeled robots bowing their heads with serene expressions and reciting perfect prayers. He wants real life children to come to Him with their problems. To lay their burdens before Him. To speak with utmost honesty, even in anger, even through tears of frustration. In that place of honesty, He can meet us powerfully, soothe our pain, and encourage us.

You will either draw near to Him with your questions or pull away in bitterness.

Believe me, He is big enough to handle your questions.

I remember asking God all sorts of questions when I was stuck in that hospital.

"God, WHY? Why me? Why is this happening? Do You not like me?"

As a father of four, I want my kids to come to me and ask me why I don't do certain things. When I don't do something they want and it's hard for them, I want them to come to me and ask, "Daddy, why won't you give this to me? Why won't you do this for us?"

Some might see this as disrespect. But to me, it's a sign of intimacy. If my kids feel they can never ask me such questions, they'll turn away and seek answers elsewhere. I want my kids to draw near to me their whole lives.

People of God, draw near to Him. Don't pull away. He's waiting to hear every single question you have on your mind. He wants access to the depths of your hearts, not your shallow and skin-deep facade of religious performance.

Still, Martha didn't stop with her questions. She hadn't lost her faith. "But I know even now God will give You whatever You ask," she said.

She had asked Jesus why, but she still knew He was good. This is the key piece in our honesty with God: We can bring all our questions to God—but let them be undergirded with unshakable trust in His goodness. He is our Father, who loves us far more than we can even begin to comprehend. In your honesty, do not forget this. Questioning God without trusting His character can quickly sink into accusation.

Jesus did not hesitate a moment in His response to Martha.

"Jesus said to her, 'Your brother will rise again.' Martha answered, 'I know he'll rise again in the resurrection on the last day.' Jesus said to her, 'I am the resurrection and the life. The one who believes in me will live, even though they die. And whoever lives by believing in me will never die. Do you believe this?' She said to Him, 'Yes, Lord; I believe that You are the Christ, the Son of God, who is coming into the world.'"
- John 11:23-27

Way to go Martha! You nailed it.

Even in our darkest hour we have a reason to celebrate, because we know that death is not the end for us. If you have given your life to Jesus, there is always hope. Because although this life on earth might stink at times, we know we are promised eternal life in heaven with Jesus in paradise. That's the whole reason Jesus died! He took all of our sin, all our darkness, all our hopelessness and despair, and brought us into glorious light. When He died on the cross, carrying the sin of the world on His shoulders, its power was broken. And when He rose from the dead, we were given the power to rise as well, leaving death and darkness behind forever.

Jesus defeated sin and death so that we can enter into relationship with Him forever. This means that for us, when things in life seem to crumble, when everything seems to be going wrong, we can still say, "But you know what? I'm going to heaven. I'm not going to hell. I'm gonna be in eternal celebration forever. Ha!"

That's a reason to celebrate, despite my pain.

The world doesn't have that. So many people remain in darkness without Jesus. If you have never given your life to Jesus, let's nail that down right now. Don't wait another moment. He's here for you. The Bible says, *"If you confess with your mouth that Jesus is Lord and believe in your heart that God raised Him from the dead, you will be saved."*

Don't wait another moment. Now is your time.

Back to the story.

"When she had said this, she went and called her sister Mary, saying in private, 'The Teacher is here and is calling for you.' And when she heard it, she rose quickly and went to Him. Now Jesus had not yet come into the village, but was still in the place where Martha had met him. When the Jews who were with her in the house, consoling her, saw Mary rise quickly and go out, they followed her, supposing that she was going to the tomb to weep there. Now when Mary came to where Jesus was and saw Him, she fell at His feet, saying to Him, 'Lord, if you had been here, my brother would not have died.' When Jesus saw her weeping, and the Jews who had come with her also weeping, He was deeply moved in His spirit and greatly troubled. And He said, 'Where have you laid him?' They said to Him, 'Lord, come and see.' Jesus wept."

- John 11:28-35

Jesus wept. Two words. The shortest verse in the Bible, and quite possibly the most revelatory statement of God's character that's ever been written. Think about it. Jesus knows what He's about to do. He knows Lazarus is about to walk out of the tomb, but still Jesus weeps. Though he knows all tears will be turned to laughter ... that the ending is going to be so good ... He still weeps in the moment of others' pain.

I believe another reason many find it hard to party is because they are overcome with grief. Tragedy has stricken. Horrible news has come. And it seems utterly impossibly for them to even begin to celebrate. Hearts are weighed down, spirits are weary. Sadly, many Christians think in order to be 'spiritual' or 'Godly' they have to stuff their grief down and put on a happy face all the time. But if you don't honestly deal with your grief, it will cause roots of bitterness in your heart against God and His people.

There's simply too much pain in the world to act like everything is okay. There is sickness, death, divorce, abuse. A myriad of pains that darken our days like storm clouds shrouding the sun. It's not just okay to grieve over these things; it's imperative. If you never truly grieve, you don't let the Lord in to heal your pain. The Bible says that God wants to give "*a garment of praise instead of a spirit of despair.*" He wants to comfort those who mourn. But if you never mourn, you can never fully know the one who comforts.

We also must be a people who can mourn with those who mourn and grieve with those who grieve. Don't just fling out trite solutions to the hurting. Be with them in their grief and pain. Cry with them. Weep with them.

When Jesus wept, He did exactly that. He saw his friends' pain, felt their grief, and cried with them. He did not tell them to stop crying or to snap out of their emotion, even though He knew what He was about to do.

"Then the Jews said, 'See how He loved him!' But some of them said, 'Could not He who opened the eyes of the blind also have kept this man from dying?' Then Jesus, deeply moved again, came to the tomb."
- John 11:36-38a

I love to picture Jesus here, fraught with emotion, as He approaches His friend's grave. He is not detached and aloof like we see Jesus in so many movies. He's not the stoic Messiah preparing for a miracle. He's the weeping Son of God, deeply affected by the pain of those around Him.

The Madsen family continued to believe for Clay's healing. But with every passing week and month, the cancer only worsened. Though so many people prayed and cried out to God, Clay eventually died, and it almost broke the community who had believed so ardently in the power of God's healing.

But after his death, something very interesting happened. One by one, Clay's friends started calling out to God and were saved. People started giving their lives to Jesus left and right. And then, after a time of grieving, Clay's parents determined not to wallow in their grief and walk away from the Lord because of what had happened.

"If God wants to do something through the situation," they said, "we want to be used by Him."

They had recently met some friends who were gifted Bible teachers and decided to partner with them to impact the community. So many people had reached out to the Madsens in their pain, now they wanted to extend the same gift to others.

They opened up their home to lead a Bible study called *Walk Thru the Bible*. They were already well-connected in the community, but through the journey of their son's sickness, they had developed friendships with hundreds, if not thousands of people. Each week, more and more people entered their home. One by one, their friends started coming to Christ. It started with ones and twos, then grew to fives and tens, and soon grew into the hundreds. At last count, they've had five thousand people go through the Bible study in their home. Two thousand of those people have come to know Jesus in a personal way.

When you ask Larry and Nancy if they still experience pain from Clay's death, they say "absolutely." But in the midst of the tragedy, God was good to them, and has used them in unexpected and amazing ways.

Abundant life in the midst of agony.

So Jesus approaches the tomb, deeply moved, and we see the miracle unfold.

"It was a cave, and a stone lay against it. Jesus said, 'Take away the stone.' Martha, the sister of the dead man, said to Him, 'Lord, by this time there will be an odor, for he has been dead four days.' Jesus said to her, 'Did I not tell you that if you believed you would see the glory of God?'"
- John 11:38b-40

If you believe, you will see the glory of God.

For those of you in trials, for those of you going through the hardest time of your lives ... if you believe, you will see the glory of God. He is so ready to show you His goodness, His mercy, and His love. Do not give in to the lie that He has abandoned you. He could no sooner abandon Himself. Though the pain feels too much to bear ... believe.

Cling to Him, for He is already holding on to you.

"So they took away the stone. And Jesus lifted up His eyes and said, 'Father, I thank you that you have heard me. I know that You always hear me. But I said this for the benefit of the people standing here, that they might believe You sent me.' When He had said these things, He cried out with a loud voice, 'Lazarus, come out.' The man who had died came out, his hands and feet wrapped with

strips of linen and cloth around his face. Jesus said to them, 'Take
off the grave clothes and let him go.'"
– John 11:41-44

Now that's a good story!

But it's not just 'once upon a time', folks. Jesus raises people from the dead. And I don't just mean in a spiritual sense either. I mean literal resurrection. I've got friends who have seen it with their very own eyes. A missionary I know named Jim Yost who serves in Indonesia has actually prayed for a dead person and seen them come alive. This is documented. On another occasion, in Mongolia, I heard of someone being raised from the dead and as a result of the miracle, an entire village came to the Lord.

Hello.

That's amazing.

Jesus raises the dead.

But let's use the story of Lazarus as an analogy for own lives. Think about these words: tomb, dead, bad odor. Some of us believe that unless we get our lives totally in order, unless we clean ourselves up perfectly, Jesus won't want anything to do with us. No! Jesus goes right into the muck and mire of our messed up lives and brings hope. He stands in the midst of our stench and decay and brings life.

He's not deterred whatsoever by your 'odor.'

He's like the ultimate Febreeze.

I know that every story doesn't resolve like Lazarus'. I know a lot of people who have died and none of them have risen from the dead. But God wants you to know that in our pain, in our sorrow, He is good. And He's working on behalf of those who love Him.

Romans 8:28 says, *"We know that in all things, God works for the good of those who love Him and have been called according to His purpose."*

Men and women, I can't tell you why bad things happen in your life. And I can't promise your circumstances will change. I can't even tell you that God will answer your prayers exactly the way you want. But this is what you can stand on: In the midst of your pain, in the midst of your trouble ... when you don't want to party ... you have a good God. One who is working out all of your circumstances, even the bad ones, for your good.

If that's not a reason to party, I don't know what is.

9

IT ALL ENDS WITH A PARTY

In 1999 a young woman named Jennie Riddle prayed a simple prayer: God, help me write a song that the angels and all of creation are already singing so that we could join in with one voice, as one bride, to one King.

What resulted was a melody that had the 'sound of heaven.' Over and over, the song played in her head as notes and lyrics crystalized. "When I sang it, the Lord began to speak," she described later. "I can still hear the Lord whispering to me that He would carry this song across the world."

Initially she marveled over the fact that a song she had written might be sung by some of her missionary friends overseas to natives in the bush. But Jennie had no idea that this song, Revelation Song, would eventually become a global phenomenon. In 2010 it was the Dove Worship Song of the Year, reaching number one on the Christian music charts and remained there for several weeks. For months it was the most downloaded song by worship leaders worldwide.

Because it was straight out of scripture.

Before writing the song, Jennie had been meditating on

Revelation chapter four, one of the most beautiful depictions ever put to the page.

"After this I looked, and there before me was a door standing open in heaven. And the voice I had first heard speaking to me like a trumpet said, 'Come up here, and I will show you what must take place after this.' At once I was in the Spirit, and there before me was a throne in heaven with someone sitting on it. And the one who sat there had the appearance of jasper and ruby. A rainbow that shone like an emerald encircled the throne. Surrounding the throne were twenty-four other thrones, and seated on them were twenty-four elders. They were dressed in white and had crowns of gold on their heads. From the throne came flashes of lightning, rumblings and peals of thunder. In front of the throne, seven lamps were blazing. These are the seven spirits of God. Also in front of the throne there was what looked like a sea of glass, clear as crystal. In the center, around the throne, were four living creatures, and they were covered with eyes, in front and in back. The first living creature was like a lion, the second was like an ox, the third had a face like a man, the fourth was like a flying eagle. Each of the four living creatures had six wings and was covered with eyes all around, even under its wings. Day and night they never stop saying: 'Holy, holy, holy is the Lord God Almighty, who was, and is, and is to come.' Whenever the living creatures give glory, honor and thanks to him who sits on the throne and who lives for ever and ever, the twenty-four elders fall down before him who sits on the throne and worship him who lives for ever and ever. They lay their crowns before the throne and say: 'You are worthy, our Lord and God, to receive glory and honor and power, for you created all things, and by your will they were created and have their being.'"
 - *Revelation 4:1-11*

This is the center of the universe.

It's not the White House.

It's not Hollywood.

It's a throne in heaven.

But what is it about this setting that proves so intriguing? I believe it's because the image contains several key things that capture our hearts. Let me break it down.

There's a voice like a trumpet blast.

As humans, we are captivated by music. When songs are played beautifully, with excellence, something stirs within us like fire. Our ears were created to receive each note with delight. And in heaven, music will play an eternal role. I'm a sucker for all kinds of music, always have been. But I know that when I get to heaven, and the angel Gabriel pulls out his electric guitar, the music will be so good it will melt my face off.

And then I'll get a new one.

There's a throne.

Most of us are innately inspired by royalty. Why else do we tune in to royal weddings on the other side of the ocean? Why else do we care one wit about the royal baby? There is simply something within us that is drawn to regality, to nobility. This is not Jesus walking down dusty paths on earth, this is Jesus on a throne by a sea of glass. His skin is not a normal shade, but shining like jewels. What human is not captivated by precious stones? Jesus' very form shines like a treasure trove.

There's a rainbow.

The one in this picture encircles the throne like a kaleidoscopic crown.

Twenty-four thrones with twenty-four elders.

I like to imagine these guys like Gandalf, two-dozen wizened sages surrounding Jesus on all sides. But every time the words,

'Holy, holy, holy,' come forth, they fall flat on their faces in worship. The wisest, most regal people on earth cannot stand in the presence of God. Even with their sheer white robes and golden crowns, they lay all before the King.

Flashes of lightning.

Some friends of mine were recently on a trip up into the mountains and they sent me a video of an electrical storm. The sky was awash with brilliant webs of light. But what I enjoyed more than watching flashes of lighting on the video was the sound of their response when a flash would whiten the sky. Their whole car was all, 'Oooohhh' and 'Aahhhhhh' in perfect synchrony with the lightning, followed by booming thunder like the pounding of a great drum. These same things emanate from the throne of God. Mind blowing.

Lamps of fire.

I'm a self-proclaimed pyromaniac. Most humans are, whether they admit it or not. We love to stare into the glowing coals of a campfire. We love to light candles. We even buy DVDs of crackling fires to play on our TVs for the mere sake of ambiance. I recently went camping with my kids and for the life of me, I couldn't keep them away from the fire. Mountains and forests surrounded us, but all they wanted to do was throw things into the flames to watch them burn. What is it about fire? Maybe it's because it speaks of the transcendent glory of God.

A sea as clear as crystal.

Why are oceanfront properties so exorbitantly expensive? It's because we are drawn to vast expanses of water. We love to sit upon the beach as waves crash in rhythm onto sand. We listen to the sounds, breathe the salt-tinted air, gaze mesmerized into the hazy distance where water meets sky. The ocean speaks of the majesty and massiveness of God.

The living creatures.

If I'm honest here, these things kind of freak me out. I mean they have eyes *everywhere*. Not only does this seem anatomically impossible, but it sounds straight out of a sci-fi movie. So, why do they have so many eyes in so many places? Let me theorize for a moment. Two eyes are not enough, for one cannot get enough of God. Each uniquely placed eyeball was there to behold God more fully. In the same way, He wants to fascinate you. To enamor you. To captivate the core of your being. The more you see Him, the more this will happen.

This scene is marked with a worship song: *Holy, Holy Holy, is the Lord God Almighty*. And how I wish I could hear the sound, see the colors, feel the electric presence of the glory of God.

When John saw this in Revelation chapter one he said, "*I fell on my face as though dead.*"

Have you ever been so awestruck by something that it knocks you on your face as though dead? Me neither. That's big time. But someday, we're going to be. This is our destiny, to stand before the throne of God so riveted we can hardly stay on our feet.

Did you notice something else surrounding the throne?

Something captivating, and majestic.

The most beautiful portrait of humanity.

Around the throne of God ... is a party.

In this final chapter, we're going to talk about the party to end all parties. A celebration of such magnitude, nothing can compare to it since the beginning of time.

God is going to bring the nations around His throne.

"After this I looked and there before me was a great multitude that no one could count from every nation, tribe, people, and language, standing before the throne and before the Lamb."
- Revelation 7:9

139

In human history, there's only been one event that can remotely come close to such a gathering. In 2008, the world witnessed the single greatest viewed event of all mankind, seen by over one billion people worldwide through television ... the opening ceremony of the Olympics Games in Beijing, China. While the Olympic torch was brought into the arena to ignite the massive flame, athletes from almost every nation on the planet paraded in a vast circle, hoisting their flags, faces beaming.

But did you know there will come a day when people from *every* nation will gather around a throne, where the fire of God blazes, to worship for eternity? And there will be far more than a mere billion people. The Bible says that *every eye* will see Him.

When we understand God's heart for every kindred nation, tribe, and tongue, we begin to tap in to the longings of heaven, God's passion to see His people redeemed and gathered to Himself.

Years ago, while studying in England during one college summer, my classmates and I would take "the tube" under the city to various locations. I was amazed how each stop offered such vastly different scenery. One particular evening, as we climbed the stairs out of the underground station, we found our-selves in the middle of Piccadilly Circus.

Instantly I was enamored by the lights, the sounds, the smells, and the colors. Everything converged on the senses. As we ambled amidst the crowd, I noticed different groups walking together along the way. First, I saw a cluster of Africans with their vibrant colored clothing. Then I noticed a number of Middle-Eastern Muslims with their elaborate head coverings of red and white and black. Beyond them was a group of Chinese tourists, each clutching a camera and snapping pictures like mad. A Peruvian wood flute band made music on the side of the road as we passed. There were Gypsies here, and neon-haired punk rockers there.

Homeless people meandering around. A stunning, kaleidoscopic montage of humanity coming together in one little square.

Then, somewhere away from the bulk of the crowds, I heard music playing. Slowly, people began to move in the sound's direction. I followed behind until I could see a group of musicians in matching t-shirts.

They were singing songs about Jesus.

People of all languages and backgrounds listened silently as each song seemed to wash over the crowd like water. I stood there for some time until I noticed a skirmish erupting nearby. A disgruntled drunk man was confronting an older gentleman, and cursing at the top of his lungs. It was clear that the older man was the leader of the group who had come to sing about Jesus. Straining to hear what was being said, I witnessed something remarkable.

The older man, instead of reacting to the verbal attack, simply looked at the drunk with eyes of love and compassion and told him that Jesus loved him.

At that moment, as I stared at the scene, surrounded by people of all different nationalities, I felt like God whispered to me: *This is My dream for the Church. That My Church would be in the midst of every kindred nation, tribe, and tongue.*

When I tell people about the birth of our church here in San Diego, I say we were planted in 2008, but God put the seed of *All Peoples Church* in 1997, in that square of Piccadilly Circus. It was there I felt God's heart for the nations for the very first time.

The Bible talks about a city whose foundation is the Lord.

And that's our ultimate destination.

"Then I heard what sounded like a great multitude, like the roar of rushing waters and loud peals of thunder, shouting: 'Halleluja! For our Lord God Almighty reigns. Let us rejoice and be

glad and give Him glory! For the wedding of the Lamb has come, and His bride has made herself ready. Fine linen, bright and clean, was given her to wear.' (Fine linen stands for the righteous acts of God's holy people.) Then the angel said to me, 'Write this: Blessed are those who are invited to the wedding supper of the Lamb!' And he added, 'These are the true words of God.'"

- *Revelation 19:6-9*

Our time on earth culminates with a party.

It's called The Wedding Supper of the Lamb.

And you are invited.

Some people might be wondering what in the world I'm talking about. So, the end of the world involves a meal and a little sheep? Not too exciting. But let's dig a little deeper to see what's really going on here.

The "lamb" is a symbolic reference. It represents something. We've all got these kinds of things in our day to day lives. I call my wife 'honey.' It's not because she's made up of some sweet, amber goo and goes great on a biscuit with a pat of butter. It's a symbol. To me, she's like honey. She's sweet. She's delightful. You get the picture.

Jesus is the lamb.

But why choose a lamb? I mean, He's the Son of God. Shouldn't His mascot at least be a little more formidable? Maybe be a tiger, or a lynx, or something powerful? Well, the people of God at the time this was written had a greater understanding of what a lamb represented. Lambs actually played a crucial role in their faith. Let me explain.

God is perfect. God is sinless. God is without fault. But we as His people have sin in our lives. I'm sure none of us would disagree. And the Bible says that the *"wages of sin is death."* So where does the lamb come in? God didn't want His children to die in their sins. He loves us far too much. So back in the day, He instructed His people, in preparation for every Passover celebration, to take a spotless, unblemished lamb and bring it into their home. They were to nurture it like a beloved pet, then at the end of three days, they were to kill it. To spill its blood.

Wow. So inspiring.

Bear with me here.

Why kill this innocent, fluffy little creature? Why take the life of something that had done absolutely nothing to deserve such a punishment? The lamb died on behalf of the people. It paid the price for their sins.

When Jesus came onto the scene, He was described as *"The Lamb of God, who takes away the sin of the world."*

Jesus, like the lamb, was pure. He never sinned. He lived a perfect life. All He did was love. All He did was draw people through His compassion. Yet, He was nailed to a cross in one of the most painful deaths imaginable. His blood was spilled. Why?

For us.

His act of willful sacrifice was the final payment for our sins. The ultimate rescue. He became the scapegoat, suffering a criminal's fate, for us. And as a result, God put Him *on the throne.*

The Lamb of God reigns.

And those who are washed clean by what He did for us are invited to a party. And when we arrive at this party, God will join us with Jesus in a covenant forever.

This is our destiny.

Because God loves us. God loves you.

If we would even scratch the surface of the measure of His love, our hearts could not possibly resist Him.

He loved us long before we loved Him.

And nothing can change that.

So how will it all end?

"Then I saw a great white throne and Him who was seated on it. And the earth and the heavens fled from His presence, and there was no place for them. And I saw the dead, great and small, standing before the throne, and books were opened. Another book was opened, which is the book of life. And the dead were judged according to what they had done as recorded in the books. The sea gave up the dead that were in it and death and Hades gave up the dead that were in them, and each person was judged according to what they had done. Then death and Hades were thrown into the lake of fire. The lake of fire is the second death. Anyone whose name was not found written in the book of life was thrown into the lake of fire.

Then I saw 'A new heaven and a new earth,' for the first heaven and the first earth had passed away, and there was no longer any sea. And I saw the Holy City, the new Jerusalem, coming down out of heaven from God, prepared as a bride beautifully dressed for her husband. And I heard a loud voice from the throne saying, 'Look! God's dwelling is now among the people, and He will dwell with them. They will be His people, and God Himself will be their God.

"He will wipe every tear from their eyes. There will be no more death" or mourning or crying or pain, for the old order of things has passed away'.

He who was seated on the throne said, 'I am making everything new!'"

- Revelation 20:11-21:5a

We are headed to a party where there is no more death.

No more pain.

No more tears.

All the suffering we endure on the earth will be over and done.

Defeated. Vanquished. Gone forever.

No more cancer. No more AIDS. No more famine.

No more genocide. No more war.

Molestation? Gone.

Abuse? Gone.

Addiction? Gone.

No more despair.

The end of all darkness begins at the party.

Where Jesus wipes away every tear and makes all things new. All. Things. New.

Our minds will be restored. Our long fought battles put to rest. We will no longer wake up in the morning and face the same old insecurities, the same old fears. Life will no longer be a cloud of weariness and dread. We will no longer be depressed or discouraged.

Because He's making all things new.

This isn't some kind of fairy tale. Some kind of pipe dream made up by overzealous pastors. This is in the Bible, folks! The Word of God. It's going to happen. Period.

And for us, whose destiny lies before the glorious throne of God forever ... there is only one fitting response.

Celebration!

It's joining in with the heavenly host and saying, "Hallelujah! Salvation! Glory! Power! Belong to our God!"

The party to end all parties.

Forever and ever.

Amen.

MORE PRODUCTS FROM

CLEAR DAY PUBLISHING

For more information

Visit: Cleardaymediagroup.com

REALIGN
FINDING GOD'S PURPOSE FOR YOUR MONEY
Book by Josh Lawson

Would you like to have a closer walk with God in every area of your life, including finances?

God knows what it will take for you to experience the satisfaction that comes from finding purpose for your money - His purpose. In REALIGN, you'll go beyond the surface level symptoms, discovering the deeper issues that cause you problems, and realign your life.

Available at: Cleardaypublishing.com, **amazon**.com, **Christianbook.com** 1-800-CHRISTIAN, and wherever fine books are sold.

MORE THAN ANOTHER FINANCIAL COURSE

A BRAND NEW & DIFFERENT FINANCIAL CURRICULUM

REALIGN focuses not only on the "nuts and bolts" of financial planning, but also emphasizes the spiritual aspects of money matters. REALIGN deals with the whole person, from the inside out, not simply finances. The power of this 8 week course is found in the fact that God is brought into every decision a person makes. The goal: to give every person a closer walk with God by allowing Him into financial decisions.

REALIGNCLASS.COM

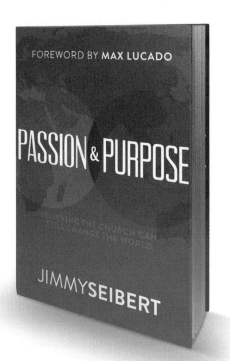

PASSION & PURPOSE
BELIEVING THE CHURCH CAN STILL CHANGE THE WORLD

Passion & Purpose is a book about the people of God – His Church – passionately pursuing Him and being deeply committed to His purposes. Nothing more. Nothing less. But the results are changing the world. The dramatic stories in this book of God's power, interventions, and miracles, will ignite or reignite your passion for Jesus and His purposes.

"To visit Antioch Community Church is to visit the book of Acts."
  - Max Lucado

Available at: Cleardaypublishing.com, amazon.com, Christianbook.com 1-800-CHRISTIAN, and wherever fine books are sold.

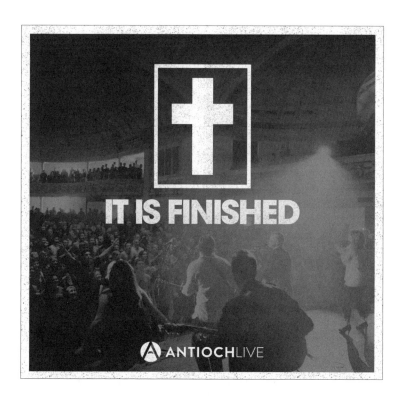

Live Worship Album by
ANTIOCHLIVE

Available on iTunes, Amazon and at ClearDayWorship.com

facebook.com/antiochlive
Antiochcc.com
ClearDayWorship.com